THE BOOK OF DASH

THE BOOK OF DASH

Build Dashboards with Python and Plotly

by Adam Schroeder, Christian Mayer, and Ann Marie Ward

no starch
press

San Francisco

Printed in the United States of America

First printing

26 25 24 23 22   1 2 3 4 5

ISBN-13: 978-1-7185-0222-2 (print)
ISBN-13: 978-1-7185-0223-9 (ebook)

Publisher: William Pollock
Managing Editor: Jill Franklin
Production Manager: Sabrina Plomitallo-González
Production Editor: Jennifer Kepler
Developmental Editor: Liz Chadwick
Cover Illustrator: Gina Redman
Interior Design: Octopod Studios
Technical Reviewer: Tom Begley
Copyeditor: Audrey Doyle
Production Services: Westchester Publishing Services
Proofreader: Rachel Head
Indexer: BIM Creatives, LLC

For information on distribution, bulk sales, corporate sales, or translations, please contact No Starch Press, Inc. directly at info@nostarch.com or:

No Starch Press, Inc.
245 8th Street, San Francisco, CA 94103
phone: 1.415.863.9900
www.nostarch.com

Library of Congress Control Number: 2022020454

To Isabel, my beloved wife.
—Adam

About the Authors

Adam Schroeder has been teaching Plotly Dash for over two years on YouTube as *@CharmingData*. His videos have over 60,000 views per month. Adam is passionate about helping people learn data visualization. He has an MA in government and conflict resolution and works for Plotly.

Christian Mayer has a PhD in computer science and is the founder of the popular Python site Finxter.com, an educational platform that helps more than 5 million people a year learn to code. He has published a number of books, including the Coffee Break Python series, and is the author of *Python One-Liners* (No Starch Press, 2020) and *The Art of Clean Code* (No Starch Press, 2022).

Ann Marie Ward is a Dash contributor and a moderator on the Dash community forum. Ann Marie has a BA in economics and is a retired CEO. She discovered Dash when searching for a better way to analyze financial data and was so amazed by what's possible to create with Dash that she started to learn Python, JavaScript, and R. Her contributions to Dash include improving documentation, fixing bugs, and adding features.

About the Technical Reviewer

Tom Begley is a data scientist and the co-creator and maintainer of dash-bootstrap-components. He has a PhD in mathematics and five years of experience working as a data scientist in industry. He discovered Dash when looking for ways to build interactive data visualizations for his clients, and has since become an active contributor to the Dash community and ecosystem.

BRIEF CONTENTS

CONTENTS IN DETAIL

PART II: BUILDING APPLICATIONS   43

4
FIRST DASH APP   45

5
GLOBAL DATA ANALYSIS: ADVANCED LAYOUTS AND GRAPHS   71

6
INVESTMENT PORTFOLIO: BUILDING LARGER APPS   95

7
EXPLORING MACHINE LEARNING   123

8
TIPS AND TRICKS 153

APPENDIX
PYTHON BASICS 165

INDEX 183

ACKNOWLEDGMENTS

Putting together a programming book like this is a group effort that builds on the ideas and contributions of many people.

First and foremost, we want to thank *you*, the reader, for spending your valuable time with us. Our main goal is to make reading this book worth your while and, hopefully, get you as excited as we are about creating your own dashboard applications.

We would also like to thank the Plotly Dash community members for making the Plotly forum a thriving place. Over the years, we've learned a lot from the forum and honed our Dash skills thanks to the curiosity and constant support of the community.

Our deep gratitude goes to the wonderful team at No Starch Press for making the book writing process such a delightful experience. Special thanks to our outstanding editor, Liz Chadwick, for being there for us throughout the project. Liz truly is a one-of-a-kind editor, and we're very lucky to have had her support! Jennifer Kepler, our production editor, pushed this book from rough draft to final publication, which was not an easy endeavor—thanks a million, Jennifer! Our technical reviewer, Tom Begley, helped us significantly improve this book by contributing his impressive technical programming and Dash expertise. Moreover, we're thankful to Bill Pollock, founder of No Starch Press, for believing in our project and allowing us to contribute to his inspiring mission to educate more coders.

Lastly, we're very grateful to our beloved partners for enduring the long night and weekend shifts to work on this project.

And with that, let's get started!

INTRODUCTION

Information is power, some say. Data is the new gold, others proclaim. But raw information and data are often meaningless without context. Data is a valuable asset only when properly analyzed, interpreted, and understood. As a result, new fields proliferate. Data scientist, data engineer, data analyst, business intelligence consultant, and machine learning engineer are all increasingly popular careers, and they all share a common role: interpreting data using visual tools such as graphs and dashboards.

The goal of this book is to help you create beautiful dashboard apps so that you can visualize your data with just a few lines of code. Whether you're an aspiring professional, you work with data on a regular basis, or you just love to play with numbers, this book will give you the tools and education to harness the power of data.

Why This Book

The Plotly Dash framework makes it super easy for you to build your own dashboards. *Dashboards* are web apps that allow you and your users to dynamically explore data using interactive widgets that receive user input to explain output. For example, they might have sliders, text fields, buttons, and dropdown menus to allow the user to choose what data to show in the resultant charts and graphs, like the maps and bar charts you see in Figure 1. The interactivity of dashboard apps is what has made them increasingly popular in recent years.

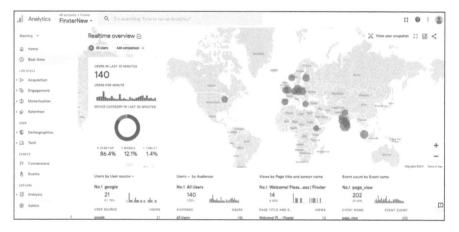

Figure 1: Google Analytics dashboard to track website usage

Building a Plotly Dash app without proper guidance can be hard. This book will teach you how to create your first interactive, highly visual analytical dashboard apps using practical instructions and easy-to-understand tutorials. It will guide you from absolute Dash beginner to creating your own dashboard apps quickly and confidently.

Reading this book will also help you hone crucial 21st-century skills including programming, data analysis, and data science, as well as data visualization and presentation. The community is hungry for stunning data visualizations of dynamic and growing datasets, generated by myriads of data sources such as smart homes, factories, web stores, social networks, video hosting services, and health tracking devices.

As the scale and complexity of data proliferate, we'll see a growing need for dashboard applications that can provide users with a real-time, data-driven overview of what's happening in the world. Chances are you've already used browser-based dashboards in your own life: Google Analytics, Facebook Ad Manager, and Salesforce Dashboards are some examples of real-life dashboard applications. Figure 1 shows a screenshot of the Google Analytics dashboard app that lets you track real-time website traffic.

This dashboard shows us that, at the time the screenshot was recorded, most users in the United States and Asia were still sleeping while users in Europe were already busy searching the web. How seamlessly these insights arise when visualizing the data properly using a dashboard app! Creating these types of applications has been possible only for skilled coders and large organizations that were able to connect real-time data sources with dynamic websites to create the unique value proposition provided by dashboard apps.

Figure 2 shows a screenshot of the Johns Hopkins dashboard app that visualizes the spread of COVID-19 using fresh and dynamic data streams.

Figure 2: Johns Hopkins dashboard to visualize the spread of a global disease

You can view this dashboard live at *https://coronavirus.jhu.edu/map.html*. The dashboard shows a dynamic counter that tracks the global number of cases, a map that tracks hotspots, figures on the cases per country, a progression of the spread over time, and many more static and dynamic statistics. The dashboard app is able to help hundreds of thousands of people each month get insight from data—insight they would not have obtained using only spreadsheets and tabular data.

Figure 3 shows a screenshot of an asset allocation tool created by one of the authors of this book (*https://wealthdashboard.app*).

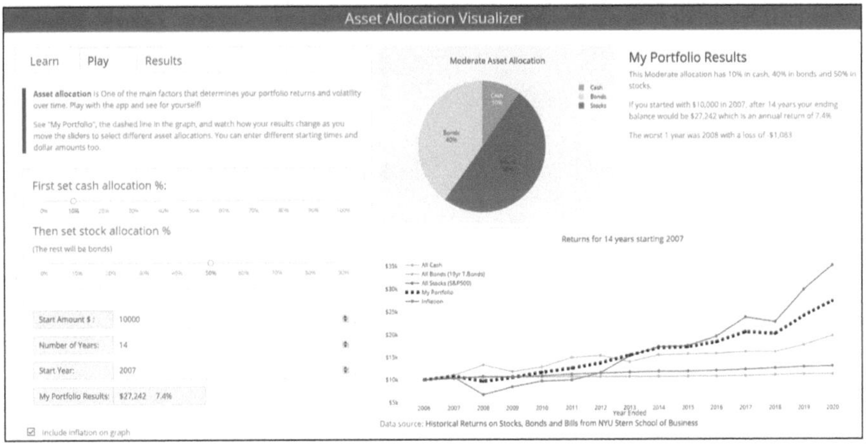

Figure 3: Wealthdashboard.com app for visualizing your asset allocation

This tool allows you to model investment returns by inputting the percentage of your wealth to allocate to stocks, bonds, and cash and using historical data to visualize key statistics on the return and risk profile of your asset allocation. This is one of the dashboards you will learn to make in this book!

The potential uses for dashboard applications are pretty much infinite. For each data source, there's a useful dashboard application waiting to be created by you.

We, the authors, have spent some sleepless nights coding and debugging and figuring out how to make our first Dash apps work. Books on Dash are rare, let alone ones that are also easy to understand and suitable for a Python beginner. So, by starting this project, we decided that it's time to change that!

Check out the many sample apps in the Dash Enterprise App Gallery at *https://dash.gallery/Portal* for more examples (see Figure 4). Some apps, like the AI Speech Recognition app, are fewer than 100 lines of code!

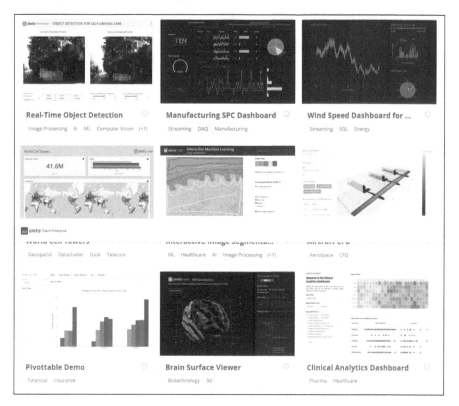

Figure 4: Screenshot of the official Dash Gallery exemplifying the many uses and features of dashboard apps

Why Plotly Dash

We've established that dashboards are great, so let's look at why you should use Plotly Dash for the job. There are a lot of great alternative frameworks for creating dashboards, including Streamlit, Shiny, Jupyter, Tableau, Infogram, and many more. However, we found a number of compelling reasons to consider Dash over its competitors in a wide variety of use cases:

- Dash apps can be written in pure Python, which means if you're familiar with Python, you'll be able to get up and running very quickly. It also means it's easy to integrate data and results from your existing Python work into a Dash app.
- Python is very expressive and Dash code can be relatively compact, meaning you're able to prototype and iterate much more quickly, which can be very useful when developing apps to a deadline or in an agile environment where requirements are regularly changing.
- Dash hides complexity from you, such as communication between the JavaScript frontend and the Python backend. So you don't need to take on overcomplicated responsibilities such as serialization, deserialization, defining API endpoints, or making HTTP requests. This can significantly reduce boilerplate code.
- Dash is developed by a Plotly team of people, meaning it has excellent integration with the Plotly graphing library. Plotly and therefore Dash are great choices for making web apps because these interactive graphs are themselves based on web technologies.
- Dash is built on top of the heavily used Flask framework, giving us many deployment options, ranging from fully managed to self-hosted.
- Although Dash can only be used with Python, it's very extensible, allowing you to mix in CSS and JavaScript, and even write your own components using React and the Dash component generator.

Although Dash has many advantages, no software is perfect. To help you decide what's best for you, here are some of Dash's limitations:

- Dash has good performance, but if you have a very large number of components, have incredibly complex apps, or are processing huge datasets, you might start to see your app slowing down.
- Dash is slightly more complicated to get up and running than some no-code or low-code alternatives, and integrations with other enterprise software are not as developed as they are with alternative frameworks; for example, PowerBI has very tight integration with Microsoft enterprise software.
- While Dash is pure Python, to properly understand what's going on, you will need to know the basics of HTML and CSS.

Who This Book Is For

We wrote this book with the total Dash beginner in mind. Although a little Python background knowledge will help you get the most out of the book, we don't assume you have a lot of programming experience, so we explain basics such as how to install Dash and related libraries, how to set up your programming environment, and how to use libraries like pandas. An entire course on Python is beyond the scope of this book, but Chapter 1 will go over some of the Python basics that are key to building Dash apps, as well as direct you to resources to help you dig in deeper where you need to.

In practice, many readers will already have some experience with the Python programming language. If you know Python but you don't have experience setting up a programming environment yet, start with Chapter 2.

If, on the other hand, you already know Python and you've set up your programming environment (preferably PyCharm), you can safely skip to Chapter 3, where we'll give you a short tutorial on the important pandas library. If you're an expert coder who knows all those things, just skip all the introductory chapters and start with Chapter 4, where we'll show you how to create your first Dash app.

What's in the Book

This book is set up in two parts: Part I will help you install and set up everything you need to build Dash apps; Part II will have you building four progressively more complex apps, and will wrap up with some general tips.

Part I: Crash Courses

Chapter 1, Python Refresher, discusses the basics of Python that are most important to building data-based apps, including data types and structures, functions, and even a little on object-oriented programming.

Chapter 2, PyCharm Tutorial, guides you through installing the PyCharm coding environment, installing libraries, creating projects, and running your Dash apps.

Chapter 3, A Crash Course in pandas, provides you with a visual overview and 10-minute recap of the pandas library for processing tabular data.

Part II: Building Applications

Chapter 4, First Dash App, shows you how to create your first Dash app using a practical example based on social media analysis. It introduces the building blocks of a Dash app, including the layout and styling sections, Dash components, callbacks, and Plotly Express for making visualizations. After reading this chapter, you'll know how to create your own basic Dash apps.

Chapter 5, Global Data Analysis: Advanced Layouts and Graphs, uses the World Bank global dataset to introduce more components and styling features. This chapter refines and expands upon your basic Dash skills: you'll interact with an API to retrieve data in real time, and learn to use dash-bootstrap-components to create more sophisticated layouts.

Chapter 6, Investment Portfolio: Building Larger Apps, dives even deeper into more advanced Dash components, using a wealth-based dashboard app as an example. You'll learn how to structure and debug larger Dash apps, use more complex Dash and Bootstrap components, and build your graphs with the lower-level Plotly Graph Objects library.

Chapter 7, Exploring Machine Learning, takes you through an app that visualizes machine learning models and gives you background about support vector machines. This shows another application of Dash: visualizing and exploring how algorithms work. You'll dig deeper into two numerical libraries often used with Dash: NumPy and scikit-learn. We'll introduce the contour plot and look at some more complex uses for Dash callbacks.

Chapter 8, Tips and Tricks, wraps up the book with the best tips and tricks and some references for further reading on topics including debugging, applying automatic formatting, making use of the Dash community, and exploring yet more apps.

Online Resources

Throughout the book, we'll recommend resources made by us, the authors, to augment your learning. There's only so much you can fit in one book, so to keep this focused, we've made plenty of code, videos, and documents available online.

- Book page with bonus material: *https://learnplotlydash.com*
- Adam's YouTube channel: *https://www.youtube.com/c/CharmingData*
- GitHub repository: *https://github.com/DashBookProject/Plotly-Dash*
- Updates from the publisher: *https://nostarch.com/python-dash*
- Free Python email academy and cheat sheets: *https://blog.finxter.com/email-academy*

PART I

CRASH COURSES

Dash builds on Python. While we don't assume that you are a Python expert by any means, we expect that you have a solid understanding of basic Python concepts and syntax. In this part, we revisit the most relevant Python, PyCharm, and pandas information you need to get the most out of this book. If you find yourself struggling with the code, we've added a "Python Basics" appendix to help you improve your Python skills a little bit before reading on. For a more comprehensive introduction, feel free to check out the thorough Python crash courses and cheat sheets provided at the Finxter email academy: *https://blog.finxter .com/email-academy.*

If you feel confident in Python and pandas and have a preferred integrated development environment (IDE) to work with, feel free to jump right into Chapter 4. If you feel you could use a quick revitalization of your Python and pandas skills or would like to set up the same Python IDE that is used throughout the book, keep reading!

1

PYTHON REFRESHER

If you're looking to work on Dash apps, you probably already know at least a little bit of Python. This book doesn't assume you're an expert, however, so here we'll review some important Python concepts that are more relevant to working with Dash, including lists, dictionaries, object-oriented programming, and decorator functions. If you're already really confident in your abilities in these areas, feel free to skip to Chapter 2, which covers PyCharm, the Python IDE that we'll use throughout this book.

Lists

Let's quickly revise the most important container data type used in practically all Dash apps: Python lists! Lists are important in Dash because they are used to define the layout, they are used to incorporate Dash Bootstrap themes, and they are commonly seen inside the callback and in figures built by Plotly.

The list container type stores a sequence of elements. Lists are mutable, meaning you can modify them after they've been created. Here we create a list named lst and print its length:

```
lst = [1, 2, 2]
print(len(lst))
```

Our output is simply:

```
3
```

We create a list using square brackets and comma-separated elements. Lists can hold arbitrary Python objects, duplicate values, and even other lists, so they are among the most flexible container types in Python. Here we populated our list lst with three integer elements. The len() function returns the number of elements in a list.

Adding Elements

There are three common ways to add elements to a list that already exists: appending, inserting, and concatenation.

The append() method places its argument at the end of the list. Here's an example of appending:

```
lst = [1, 2, 2]
lst.append(4)
print(lst)
```

This will print:

```
[1, 2, 2, 4]
```

The insert() method inserts an element at a given position and moves all subsequent elements to the right. Here's an example of inserting:

```
lst = [1, 2, 4]
lst.insert(2,2)
print(lst)
```

This prints the same result:

```
[1, 2, 2, 4]
```

And finally, concatenation:

```
print([1, 2, 2] + [4])
```

We get:

```
[1, 2, 2, 4]
```

For concatenation, we use the plus (+) operator. This creates a new list by gluing together two existing lists.

All operations generate the same list, [1, 2, 2, 4]. The append operation is the fastest because it neither has to traverse the list to insert an element at the correct position as inserting does, nor has to create a new list out of two sublists as concatenation does.

To append multiple elements to a given list, use the extend() method:

```
lst = [1, 2]
lst.extend([2, 4])
print(lst)
```

The code changes the existing list object lst as follows:

```
[1, 2, 2, 4]
```

The preceding code is an example of a list that's able to hold duplicate values.

Removing Elements

We can remove an element x from a list with lst.remove(x), like so:

```
lst = [1, 2, 2, 4]
lst.remove(1)
print(lst)
```

This gives us the result:

```
[2, 2, 4]
```

This method operates on the list object itself—no new list is created, and the original list is altered.

Reversing Lists

You can reverse the order of the list elements using the method lst.reverse():

```
lst = [1, 2, 2, 4]
lst.reverse()
print(l)
```

This prints:

```
[4, 2, 2, 1]
```

Reversing the list also modifies the original list object rather than creating a new list object.

Sorting Lists

You can sort the list elements using the method `lst.sort()`:

```
lst = [2, 1, 4, 2]
lst.sort()
print(lst)
```

We see the sorted list:

```
[1, 2, 2, 4]
```

Again, sorting the list modifies the original list object. The resultant list is sorted in ascending order by default. To sort in descending order, you pass `reverse=True`, as shown here:

```
lst = [2, 1, 4, 2]
lst.sort(reverse=True)
print(lst)
```

And we see the result is in reverse order:

```
[4, 2, 2, 1]
```

You can also specify a key function and pass it as the parameter key to `sort()` to customize the sorting behavior. The key function simply transforms one list element into an element that is sortable. For example, it might transform an unsortable object such as a Dash component into a sortable type by using the Dash component's string identifier as a key. Generally, these key functions allow you to sort lists of custom objects; for example, sorting a list of staff objects by their age. The following example sorts the list but uses the inverse, negative value of an element as a key:

```
lst = [2, 1, 4, 2]
lst.sort(key=lambda x: -x)
print(lst)
```

This gives us:

```
[4, 2, 2, 1]
```

The key of element 4 is the negative value -4, which is the smallest value among all list elements. Because the list is sorted in ascending manner, this is the first value of the resultant sorted list.

Indexing List Elements

You can determine the index of a specified list element x using the method `list.index(x)`, like so:

```
print([2, 2, 4].index(2))
print([2, 2, 4].index(2,1))
```

The method `index(x)` finds the first occurrence of the element x in the list and returns its index.

You can specify a starting index by passing a second argument that sets the index from which to start the search. Consequently, while the first line prints the index of the first occurrence of the value 2, the second line prints the index of the first occurrence of the value 2 but starts the search from index 1. The method immediately finds the value 2 in both cases and prints:

```
0
1
```

INDEXING BASICS

Here's a quick overview of indices in Python, by example. Suppose we have the string `'universe'`. The indices are simply the positions of the characters of this string, starting at 0:

Index	0	1	2	3	4	5	6	7
Character	u	n	i	v	e	r	s	e

The first character has index 0, the second character has index 1, and the i-th character has index i-1.

Slicing

Slicing is the process of carving out a substring from a given string. We call that substring a *slice*. The slicing notation is as follows:

```
string[start:stop:step]
```

The `start` argument is the index at which we want to start the string and is included in the slice, and `stop` is the index at which we want the string to stop and is excluded from the slice. Forgetting that the `stop` index is excluded is a common source of bugs, so bear it in mind. The `step` argument tells Python which elements to include, so a `step` of 2 would include every other element and a `step` of 3 would include every third element. Here's an example with a step size of 2:

```
s = '----p-y-t-h-o-n----'
print(s[4:15:2])
```

This will give us:

```
python
```

All three arguments are optional, so you can skip them to use the default values of start=0, stop=len(string), and step=1. Leaving out the start argument before the slicing colon indicates that the slice starts from the first position, and leaving out the stop argument ends the slice at the final element. Leaving out the step argument assumes a step of 1. Here we skip the step argument:

```
x = 'universe'
print(x[2:4])
```

This gives us:

```
iv
```

Here we specify the start but not the stop, and give a step of 2, so we get every other character, starting at the third character and going to the end of the string:

```
x = 'universe'
print(x[2::2])
```

This gives us:

```
ies
```

If we accidentally give a stop index that overshoots the maximal sequence index, Python will just assume we meant to end the slice at the end of the original string. Here is an example:

```
word = "galaxy"
print(word[4:50])
```

This prints:

```
xy
```

Just remember that nothing unexpected happens if slicing overshoots sequence indices.

You can also provide negative integers for all three arguments. A negative index for start or stop tells Python to count from the end. For example, string[-3:] would start slicing with the third-to-last element and string[-10:-5] would start slicing with the tenth-to-last element (included) and stop with the fifth-to-last element (excluded). A negative step size means that Python slices from the right to the left. For example, string[::-1] would reverse the string and string[::-2] would take every other character, starting from the last and moving forward toward the left.

Dictionaries

The *dictionary* is a useful data structure for storing key-value pairs. We define a dictionary in curly brackets, like so:

```
calories = {'apple': 52, 'banana': 89, 'choco': 546}
```

The key comes first, followed by a colon, and then the value. The key-value pairs should be separated by commas. Here 'apple' is the first key and 52 is its value. You can access individual dictionary elements by specifying which dictionary to take the element from and specifying the key within brackets. In the following example, we compare the calories of an apple to the calories of a piece of chocolate:

```
print(calories['apple'] < calories['choco'])
```

Of course, it returns:

```
True
```

The dictionary is a mutable data structure, so you can change it after creation. For instance, you can add, remove, or update existing key-value pairs. Here we add a new key-value pair to the dictionary, storing the information that a cappuccino has 74 calories:

```
calories['cappu'] = 74
print(calories['banana'] < calories['cappu'])
```

When we assert that a cappuccino has more calories than a banana, we get:

```
False
```

We use the keys() and values() functions to access all keys and values of the dictionary. Here we check whether the string 'apple' is one of the dictionary keys and the integer 52 is one of the dictionary values. Both are in fact True:

```
print('apple' in calories.keys())
print(52 in calories.values())
```

To access all key-value pairs of a dictionary, we use the dictionary.items() method. In the following for loop, we iterate over each (key, value) pair in the calories dictionary and check whether each value is more than 500 calories. If this is the case, it prints the associated key:

```
for key, value in calories.items():
    if value > 500:
        print(key)
```

Our only result is:

```
'choco'
```

This gives us an easy way to iterate over all keys and all values in a dictionary without accessing them individually.

List Comprehension

List comprehension is a compact way of creating lists with the simple one-liner formula [expression + context]. The context tells Python which elements to add to the new list. The expression defines what to do with each of those new elements before adding them. For example, the list comprehension statement

```
[x for x in range(3)]
```

creates the new list [0, 1, 2]. The context in this example is for x in range(3), so the loop variable x takes on the three values 0, 1, and 2. The expression x is very basic in this example: it simply adds the current loop variable to the list without modification. However, list comprehensions are capable of handling far more advanced expressions.

List comprehension is often used in dashboard applications; for example, it is used to create multiple options for a dropdown menu on the fly. Here we create a list of strings—weekdays—and then use the list in a list comprehension to create a list of dictionaries. We'll use the dictionaries to create the labels and options for a Dash dropdown menu shown in Figure 1-1:

```
days = ['Mon', 'Tue', 'Wed', 'Thu', 'Fri', 'Sat', 'Sun']
options = [{'label': day, 'value': day} for day in days]
```

Figure 1-1: A Dash dropdown menu

The context is for day in days, so we iterate over each weekday 'Mon',...,
'Sun'. The expression creates a dictionary with two key-value pairs, {'label':
day, 'value': day}. This is a very concise way to create the following list of
dictionaries:

```
[{'label': 'Mon', 'value': 'Mon'}, {'label': 'Tue', 'value': 'Tue'},
{'label': 'Wed', 'value': 'Wed'}, {'label': 'Thu', 'value': 'Thu'},
{'label': 'Fri', 'value': 'Fri'}, {'label': 'Sat', 'value': 'Sat'},
{'label': 'Sun', 'value': 'Sun'}]
```

The alternative is to use a regular Python for loop, as shown in these
three lines:

```
options = []
for day in days:
    options.append({'label': day, 'value': day})
```

You create a list of dictionaries where both the label and the value are
associated with the respective day. Here the dropdown menu will show the
label 'Mon' and, if selected by the user, will associate the label with the value
'Mon' to it.

The context consists of an arbitrary number of for and if statements.
We could use an if statement within the list comprehension to filter results;
for example, we can create dropdown options with only weekdays:

```
options = [{'label': day, 'value': day} for day in days if day not in ['Sat', 'Sun']]
```

Here we use the if statement to exclude Sat and Sun from the resultant
list. It's a quicker, more concise way of writing this regular if statement
within a for loop.

Object-Oriented Programming

In Python, everything is an object. Even integer values are objects. This is
different from programming languages like C, where integers, floats, and
Booleans are primitive data types. In this way, Python is built on a rigor-
ously consistent object-oriented paradigm.

Classes and Objects

At the heart of object-oriented Python are classes. Classes are blueprints
for creating objects. A class description tells you what an object looks like
and what it can do, respectively known as the object's *data* and *functionality*.
The data is defined in *attributes*, which are variables associated with a given
object. The functionality is defined in *methods*, which are functions associated with the given object.

Let's see these concepts in action using Harry Potter examples. First
we'll make a class with attributes but no methods. Here we create a Muggle
class and make two Muggle objects from it:

```
class Muggle:
    def __init__(self, age, name, liking_person):
        self.age = age
        self.name = name
        self.likes = liking_person


Vernon = Muggle(52, "Vernon", None)
Petunia = Muggle(49, "Petunia", Vernon)
```

We create a new blueprint for Muggle objects using the keyword class. This dictates what data every Muggle object will have and what it can do. Here we say that each Muggle object should have an age, a name, and someone they like.

For every class, you must use the method __init__() to initialize the class with data. Every Muggle object will have the attributes age, name, and likes. By passing them in as arguments to the def statement, we make them required arguments when creating an object. The first value of any class method is a reference to the object itself, denoted as self. As soon as you call the initialization method in your code, Python creates an empty object you can access using the name self.

NOTE *Although the first argument is self when defining a method, you don't actually specify this argument when calling the method. Python does it for you internally.*

When you create an object from the class, the initialization method __init__ is automatically called first to instantiate a new object by using the name of the class as a function call. The calls Muggle(52, "Vernon", None) and Muggle(49, "Petunia", Vernon) create two new class objects, both defining the three attributes, shown here:

```
Muggle

    age = 52
    name = "Vernon"
    likes = None

Muggle

    age = 49
    name = "Petunia"
    likes = "Vernon"
```

You can see that these objects follow the same blueprint but are different instances of a Muggle; they have the same properties but different DNA.

From now on, these objects live in your computer's memory until Python kills them when the program terminates.

Can you see the tragic element of the story so far? Petunia likes Vernon, but Vernon likes nobody. Let's cheer this up a bit, shall we? We'll change the likes attribute for Vernon to Petunia. We can access the different attributes of an object using the name of the object, dot notation, and then the name of the attribute, like so:

```
Vernon.likes = "Petunia"
print(Vernon.likes)
```

This will print:

```
Petunia
```

Let's define the Wizard class so that we can create some wizards in our small world. This time we'll add some functionality:

```
class Wizard:
    def __init__(self, age, name):
        self.age = age
        self.name = name
        self.mana = 100

    def love_me(self, victim):
        if self.mana >= 100:
            victim.likes = self.name
            self.mana = self.mana - 100

Wiz = Wizard(42, "Tom")
```

Every Wizard object has three attributes: age, name, and mana level (how much magic power the wizard has left). The age and name attributes are set when you create a Wizard object according to the values passed in as arguments. The mana attribute is hardcoded to 100 in the __init__ method. For example, calling Wizard(42, "Tom") would set self.age to 42, self.name to "Tom", and self.mana to 100.

We also add the method love_me(), which casts a love spell on the victim. If the wizard has enough mana left, they can force the victim to love them by setting the victim's likes attribute to the caster's name. However, this only works if the mana level of the wizard is greater than or equal to 100 (self.mana >= 100). When successful, the victim's likes attribute points to the casting wizard's name and the casting wizard's mana level reduces by 100.

We've created a 42-year-old wizard named Tom. Tom is lonely and wants to be liked. Let's get Petunia and Vernon to love him. We access an object's methods using the dot notation and pass in the Petunia and Vernon objects:

```
Wiz.love_me(Petunia)
Wiz.love_me(Vernon)

print(Petunia.likes=="Tom" and Vernon.likes=="Tom")
```

Can you tell whether Tom was successful in making both Petunia and Vernon love him?

One of the most common sources of confusion in object-oriented programming is forgetting to include the self argument when defining a method. Another is that the definition of the initialization method uses the syntax __init__(), whereas you'd call the class creation method using the syntax ClassName() and not ClassName.__init__(), as you might expect. This is shown in the code where we do not call Wizard.__init__(20, 'Ron') but simply call Wizard(20, 'Ron') to create a new Wizard object.

This has been a brief overview of object-oriented programming in Python, but it's worth ensuring that you fully understand how to build classes and objects in Python.

For further information, you can check out the cheat sheet on object-oriented programming at *https://blog.finxter.com/object-oriented-programming -terminology-cheat-sheet*.

Terminology

Here we'll quickly sweep through a few key definitions in object-oriented Python.

Class   A blueprint to create objects. The class defines the data (attributes) and functionality (methods) of the objects. You can access both attributes and methods via the dot notation.

Object   A piece of encapsulated data with associated functionality that is built according to a class definition. Objects are also referred to as *instances* of a class. Often, an object is made to model a thing in the real world. For example, we might create the object Obama according to the class definition Person. An object consists of an arbitrary number of attributes and methods, encapsulated within a single unit.

Instantiation   The process of creating an object of a class.

Method   A function associated with a specific object. We define methods using the keyword def in the class definition. An object can have as many methods as you like.

Attribute   A variable used to hold data associated with a class or instance.

Class attribute   A variable that is created statically in the class definition and is shared by all objects created from that class. These are also variously known as *class variables*, *static variables*, and *static attributes*.

Dynamic attribute   An object attribute that is defined dynamically during program execution, and is not defined within any method. For example, you can simply add a new attribute my_attribute to any object o by calling o.my_attribute = 42.

Instance attribute   A variable that holds data belonging to only a single object. Other objects do not share this variable, as they do with class attributes. In most cases, you create an instance attribute x when creating the instance using the self variable name, like self.x = 42. These are also known as *instance variables*.

Inheritance   A programming concept that allows you to create new classes as modifications of existing classes by reusing some or all of the data and functionality when defining the new class. That is, class A can inherit attributes or methods from class B so that it has the same data and functionality as class B, but class A can alter the behavior or add data and methods. For example, the class Dog may inherit the attribute number_of_legs from the class Animal. In this case, you would define the inherited class Dog as follows: class Dog(Animal): followed by the body of the class.

If you have understood these terms, you can follow most discussions about object-oriented programming. Mastering object orientation is an important step toward proficiency in Python.

Decorator Functions and Annotations

Dash relies heavily on the Python concept of *decorators* or *decorator functions*, which add functionality to existing code without modifying the code itself. This is useful if you want to modify or customize, say, the output of an existing function without having to change the actual code of the function. For example, you may not have access to a function definition, but you may still want to change the behavior of the function. Decorator functions to the rescue!

Think of a decorator function as a wrapper. It takes an original function, calls it, and modifies its behavior after the fact according to the desires of the programmer. This way, you can change the behavior of a function dynamically, after the function was originally defined.

Let's start with a straightforward example. Let's define a function that prints some text to the standard output:

```
def print_text():
    print("Hello world!")

print_text()
```

The output is:

```
Hello world!
```

The function will always print the same message. Say you want to decorate this output to make it more interesting. One way is to define a new pretty_print() function; this is not yet a decorator function, because it doesn't change the behavior of another function. However, it does demonstrate wrapping another function and modifying its behavior:

```
def print_text():
    print("Hello world!")
```

```
def pretty_print():
    annotate = '+'

    print(annotate * 30)
    print_text()
    print(annotate * 30)


pretty_print()
```

Now the output looks like this:

```
++++++++++++++++++++++++++++++++
Hello world!
++++++++++++++++++++++++++++++++
```

The outer function pretty_print() calls the inner function print_text() and embellishes the result with 30 plus (+) symbols before and after the output of the inner function print_text(). Essentially, you *wrap* the result of the inner function and enrich it with additional functionality.

Decorator functions allow you to generalize code like this. For instance, you may want to pass an arbitrary inner function into your pretty_print() function so that you can use it on any Python function. Here we create a decorator function, but note that for the purposes of showing how it works, we're creating this function the long way. In a moment we'll look at the shorter way Python provides to do the same thing. Here's the long version:

```
def pretty_print_decorator(f):
    annotate = '+'

    def pretty_print():
        print(annotate * 50)
        f()
        print(annotate * 50)

    return pretty_print


def print_text():
    print("Hello world!")


def print_text_2():
    print("Hello universe!")
```

When we use it like so:

```
pretty_print_decorator(print_text)()
pretty_print_decorator(print_text_2)()
```

we'll get output like this:

```
+++++++++++++++++++++++++++++++++++++++++++++++++++
Hello world!
+++++++++++++++++++++++++++++++++++++++++++++++++++
+++++++++++++++++++++++++++++++++++++++++++++++++++
Hello universe!
+++++++++++++++++++++++++++++++++++++++++++++++++++
```

Here the decorator function takes a function as input and returns another function that modifies the behavior by wrapping its output in + symbols. You can pass any function that prints any output and create a similar function that additionally wraps the output in a series of + symbols.

This simple decorator function takes in a function object and applies some output modifications, but decorator functions can do all kinds of complicated things, such as analyze output, apply some extra logic, or filter out some undesired messages.

This is an unrealistically complicated way to build a decorator function. Because the pattern is so common, Python provides a convenient method that accomplishes the same thing with less code: you add one line of code in front of the function to be decorated. This line consists of the at symbol (@), followed by the name of a decorator function you defined earlier. Here we define the pretty_print_decorator(f) function, then apply it when we define the two print functions:

```python
def pretty_print_decorator(f):
    annotate = '+'

    def pretty_print():
        print(annotate * 50)
        f()
        print(annotate * 50)

    return pretty_print


@pretty_print_decorator
def print_text():
    print("Hello world!")

@pretty_print_decorator
def print_text_2():
    print("Hello universe!")
```

We call our two defined functions like so:

```python
print_text()
print_text_2()
```

And we should get output like this:

```
+++++++++++++++++++++++++++++++++++++++++++++++++++++
Hello world!
+++++++++++++++++++++++++++++++++++++++++++++++++++++
+++++++++++++++++++++++++++++++++++++++++++++++++++++
Hello universe!
+++++++++++++++++++++++++++++++++++++++++++++++++++++
```

You can see that the output is exactly the same as before. But this time, rather than calling the decorator function `pretty_print_factory` explicitly, such as in `pretty_print_decorator(print_text)` to decorate the existing function `print_text`, we modify the behavior of `print_text()` directly using the decorator function with the @ prefix. Each time we then call the decorated function, it is automatically passed through the decorator function. This way, we can stack arbitrarily complicated function hierarchies, each adding a new layer of complexity by decorating the output of another function.

Decorator functions are at the heart of the Dash framework. Dash provides advanced functionality that you can access by applying a decorator function that is already defined by Dash to any of your functions with the @ annotation. Dash refers to these decorator functions as *callback decorators*. You'll see plenty of these examples in the dashboard applications discussed in this book.

Summary

This was a very quick overview of some of the Python concepts that are most relevant to creating apps with Dash. If you found this difficult to follow, we recommend checking out the "Python Basics" appendix before you begin building apps.

But before we start creating dashboard applications, let's dive into the PyCharm framework we recommend you use for the book. If you're already a PyCharm expert or you have a different preferred programming environment, feel free to skip to Chapter 3.

2

PYCHARM TUTORIAL

In this chapter we'll introduce you to the PyCharm IDE. An *IDE*, short for *integrated development environment,* is a text editor that provides various tools to help you write code and has the potential to accelerate your programming productivity significantly. Modern IDEs generally have features like code highlighting, dynamic tool tips, auto-completion, syntax checking, code linters that check for style issues, version control to safeguard the history of your edits, debugging, visual aids, and performance optimization tools and profilers, to name a few.

As your Python dashboard applications grow, so will your need to aggregate all your source code in a single spot and in a single development environment. Increasing complexity quickly demands the use of an IDE. To follow along with the provided code examples in this book, we recommend you use PyCharm, an IDE specifically for Python. PyCharm is one of the most popular IDEs and is available for all operating systems. It simplifies the development of advanced applications, and the plethora of online tutorials and documentation is phenomenal for support. PyCharm also integrates well with Dash applications in that it allows you to run and debug them, install the required libraries quickly and easily, and use syntax checking and linters. However, if you have a preference for another IDE, such as VS Code, the instructions in this book will be easy to adapt.

Installing PyCharm

Let's start by downloading the latest version of PyCharm. The examples here are for the Windows operating system, but the steps are similar on macOS. If you're using Linux, you can check out the instructions to unpack and install the IDE in our PyCharm tutorial at *https://blog.finxter.com/pycharm-a-simple-illustrated-guide.* Using PyCharm is very similar across different operating systems. Go to *https://www.jetbrains.com/pycharm/download* and you should see something like Figure 2-1.

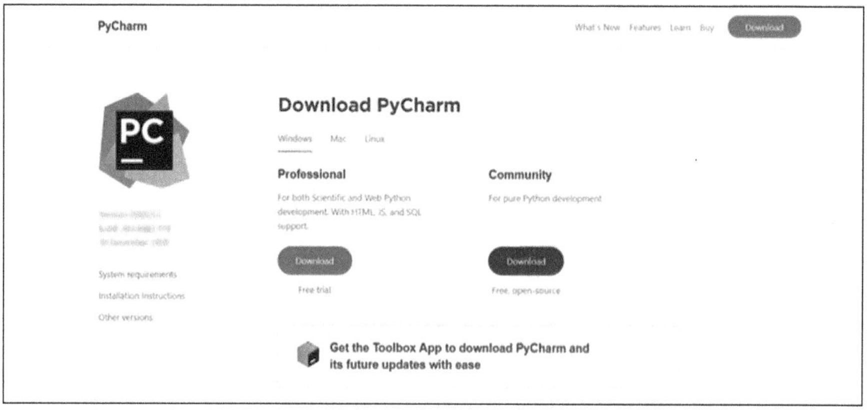

Figure 2-1: The PyCharm download page

Click **Download** for the free community version (Figure 2-1), and once it's downloaded, run the executable installer and follow the installation steps. We recommend simply accepting all the default settings suggested by the installer.

Creating a Project

Find PyCharm on your system and run it. Select **New Project**, and you should see a window similar to Figure 2-2. There are a few options in this user interface to pay attention to: a project name, which you enter as the suffix in the Location field; the virtual environment; the Python interpreter; and the checkbox for creating a *main.py* script.

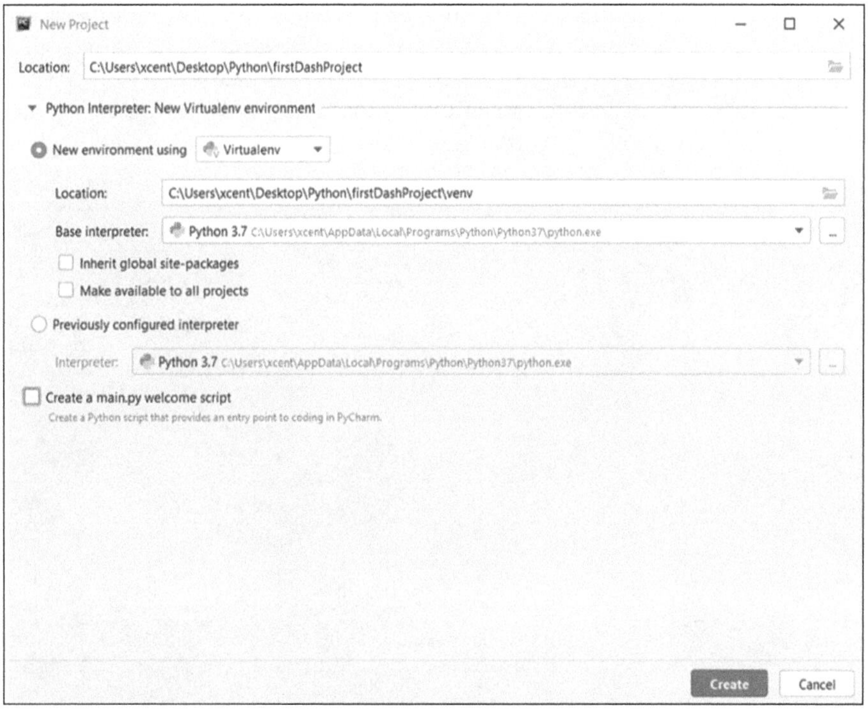

Figure 2-2: Setting up a PyCharm project

We'll call our project *firstDashProject*, but you can use any name you want. A short, all-lowercase project name would be more idiomatic, but we'll use something more obvious for the time being. To give it another name, just modify the suffix text after the last backslash (\) in the Location field.

The virtual environment and interpreter fields should auto-populate with whatever PyCharm detects on your system. In Figure 2-2, that's Python 3.7. We'll therefore use the virtual environment that comes with the standard Python installation, Virtualenv. Using a virtual environment means that all packages you install, by default, will be installed only within the project environment and not on your machine, keeping everything relevant to a project in one neat place. One of the many advantages of virtualizing your project's dependencies like this is that you can install conflicting versions for different projects without cluttering up your operating system. For example, if one project uses an older version of Dash and you need a newer version of Dash for another project, installing Dash globally will almost certainly cause problems. When you install the different Dash versions in different virtual environments—one per project—you avoid those version conflicts.

Finally, choose not to create a *main.py* welcome script by unchecking the box at the bottom. Many Python programs use *main.py* as the main entry point of their program. To execute the project, they execute the file *main.py*, which in turn kicks off all other functionality provided by the program. However, for Dash applications, the main entry point for your code is the file *app.py* per convention—although you can generally use arbitrary filenames. We therefore recommend unchecking the *main.py* box for all Dash projects.

Everything else we'll leave as it appears.

Click **Create** and you should see your first PyCharm dashboard project! It should look like Figure 2-3.

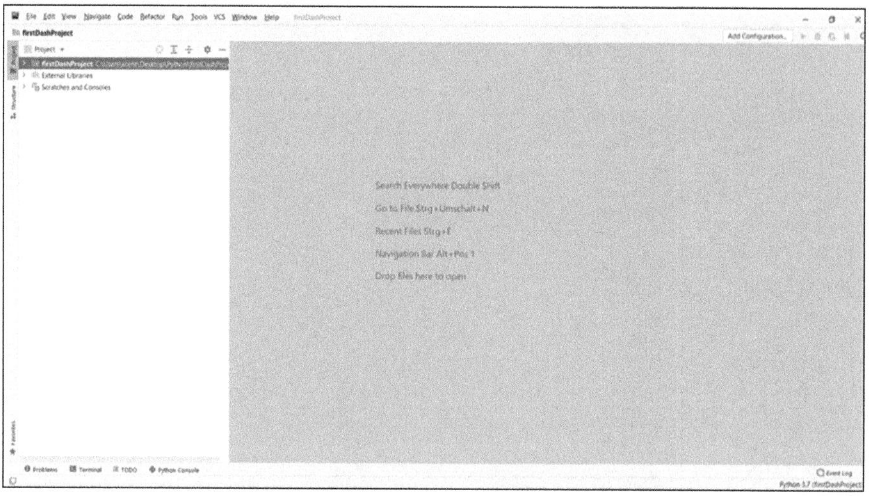

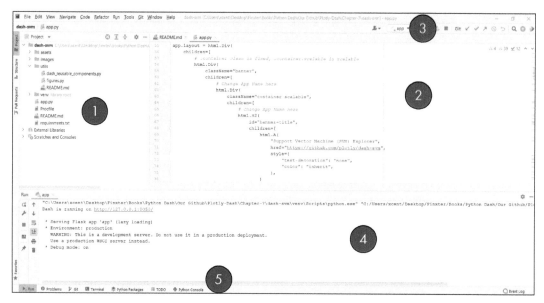

Figure 2-3: Your first PyCharm dashboard project

Before we dive into the details of how to create a dashboard application in PyCharm, let's take a quick tour of the PyCharm interface (see Figure 2-4).

Figure 2-4: Overview of the PyCharm interface

Figure 2-4 shows the most important elements of the interface:

1. The *project tool window* gives you an overview of the project folder structure. For larger projects, it's critical that you maintain a high-level overview of how all the code functions and all the modules play together to provide a coherent whole.

2. The *editor window* allows you to open, write, and edit multiple code files from your code project. You can browse the project in the project tool window and double-click files to open them in the editor window. Here's where you'll write and edit the code.

3. The *navigation bar* provides buttons and shortcuts to quickly perform the most important functions, such as starting and stopping the application, selecting the main module to be executed, searching files, and debugging your application.

4. After you've started your application, you'll observe its output and execution state in the *run tool window*. In Figure 2-4, we've just started our first dashboard application, so the run window shows the URL we can click or enter into the browser to check our dashboard application. If you use a print() statement in your code, this is where the printed output will appear.

5. The run tool window also provides another navigation bar that allows you to switch between different *tabs* of the run tool window. For example, you can open a Python shell, open a command line in Windows or the Terminal in macOS to access functionality from your operating system, or debug your application in a step-by-step manner.

PyCharm comes with a lot of additional windows, but these are the most important ones you'll use in any application, whether it's a dashboard app or not. We'll leave the rest for you to explore at your leisure.

Running a Dash App

Now we'll have a look at an example dashboard app from the official Dash documentation. This code creates the example dashboard app showing a simple bar plot graph in Figure 2-5. It also starts a server on your local computer so that you can view the dashboard app in your browser.

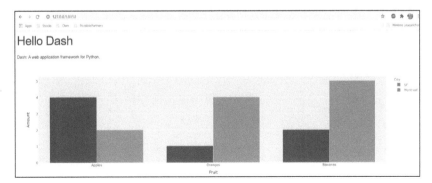

Figure 2-5: A sample Dash app

In PyCharm, right-click the project in the menu panel on the left, and select **New ▸ File**. Name your file *app.py* and copy in the code from *https://dash.plotly.com/layout*, also shown in Listing 2-1.

```python
# Run this app with 'python app.py' and
# visit http://127.0.0.1:8050/ in your web browser.

from dash import Dash, html, dcc
import plotly.express as px
import pandas as pd

import pandas as pd

# assume you have a "long-form" data frame
# see https://plotly.com/python/px-arguments/ for more options
df = pd.DataFrame({
    "Fruit": ["Apples", "Oranges", "Bananas", "Apples", "Oranges", "Bananas"],
    "Amount": [4, 1, 2, 2, 4, 5],
    "City": ["SF", "SF", "SF", "Montreal", "Montreal", "Montreal"]
})

fig = px.bar(df, x="Fruit", y="Amount", color="City", barmode="group")

app.layout = html.Div(children=[
    html.H1(children='Hello Dash'),

    html.Div(children='''
        Dash: A web application framework for your data.
    '''),

    dcc.Graph(
        id='example-graph',
        figure=fig
    )
])

if __name__ == '__main__':
    app.run_server(debug=True)
```

Listing 2-1: Example app from the Dash documentation

We don't expect you to understand this code yet, and we won't go into details now. At a very high level, this code imports the necessary libraries, builds the app and sets its style, creates the data and visualizes it in a bar plot, and sets the overall layout to include things like headings. The last two lines start the server so that you can view it in your browser (see Figure 2-6). After studying the subsequent chapters, you'll find this simple.

Now run your project: go to the top menu and select **Run ▸ app.py**. You can also click the green play button in the navigation bar. However, you'll see we've hit a snag: running the program displays an error in the run tool window at the bottom, shown in Figure 2-6. Our app doesn't yet work because we're importing Dash, but PyCharm doesn't recognize Dash! The reason is that Dash is not part of the Python standard library: you'll need to install it manually before you can use it in your project.

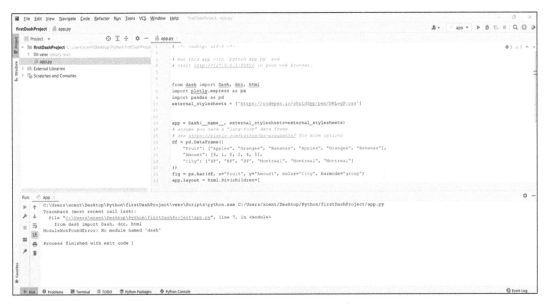

Figure 2-6: PyCharm Dash error

You may wonder why we didn't just install Dash earlier. As you'll see in a moment, because each project is isolated in its own virtual environment, this is good practice for how you'll actually use Dash in the future.

Installing Dash Through PyCharm

There are two ways to install Dash: globally on your computer, which means each future project will be able to import Dash, or locally in your virtual environment, which means only this project will be able to import Dash and you'll need to install it again for any projects in different virtual environments. The recommended way is to install it in the virtual environment.

NOTE   *PyCharm may run slightly differently on different systems, so if you run into trouble with this step, check out our full guide at* https://blog.finxter.com/how-to-install-a-library-on-pycharm *for help.*

PyCharm allows us to install Dash directly through our app code. Click the red underlined dash library import line and hover your cursor there; a small red lightbulb should appear with a menu. Choose the **Install Package Dash** option shown in Figure 2-7.

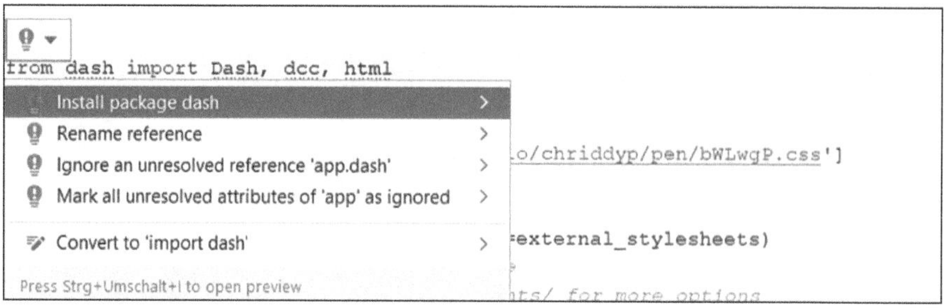

Figure 2-7: Installing Dash through PyCharm

Note that this option only appears if you have created the PyCharm project within a virtual environment (see Figure 2-2). If you don't see the package installation option, you can open the Terminal tab in your run tool window and enter:

```
$ pip install dash
```

Installing the dash library will take a few moments. It's important to remember that the library is installed only in this *virtual environment*—that is, not on your global operating system but only on a project level. For a different project, you may have to install Dash again.

Depending on your local environment, you may have to repeat the same procedure to install the pandas library as well. Visit the pandas installation guide at *https://blog.finxter.com/how-to-install-pandas-on-pycharm*. We'll cover pandas installation in Chapter 3.

Now try running *app.py* again, and you should see something like this:

```
Dash is running on http://127.0.0.1:8050/
   * Serving Flask app "app" (lazy loading)
   * Environment: production
     WARNING: This is a development server. Do not use it in a production
deployment.
     Use a production WSGI server instead.
   * Debug mode: on
```

Your app is being hosted on your local machine, so nobody can access it from the outside world. Internally, Dash uses Python's Flask library for the heavy lifting to serve the website to users. To test your application, copy *http://127.0.0.1:8050/* into your browser or click it in the output window in PyCharm. This URL indicates that the dashboard app runs on a local server hosted on your machine with IP address 127.0.0.1—this is a *loopback* address commonly referred to as *localhost* that you could read as "your local computer"—and port 8050.

For further information on PyCharm, see our multipage blog tutorial at *https://blog.finxter.com/pycharm-a-simple-illustrated-guide*.

Using Dash with GitHub

An excellent way to learn about Dash and get used to PyCharm is to copy existing Dash projects from experts and play around with their code. Studying code projects from the experts is one of the best ways to test and improve your thinking. Earlier, you tried out the example app by copying and pasting the code in the file *app.py*. This is not always the most convenient way, given that many code projects consist of multiple files and more complicated folder structures. Here we'll clone a GitHub project. Most open source projects are available on GitHub, so there are plenty for you to look at.

NOTE   *Before we begin, you'll need to have GitHub installed. If you don't, you can either download Git from the official website (https://git-scm.com/downloads) or install it through PyCharm.*

To clone a GitHub project into a new PyCharm project, first get the URL of the GitHub repository you want to clone; there are lots at *https://github.com/plotly/dash-sample-apps* to choose from. Figure 2-8 shows some sample Dash Gallery apps from Plotly.

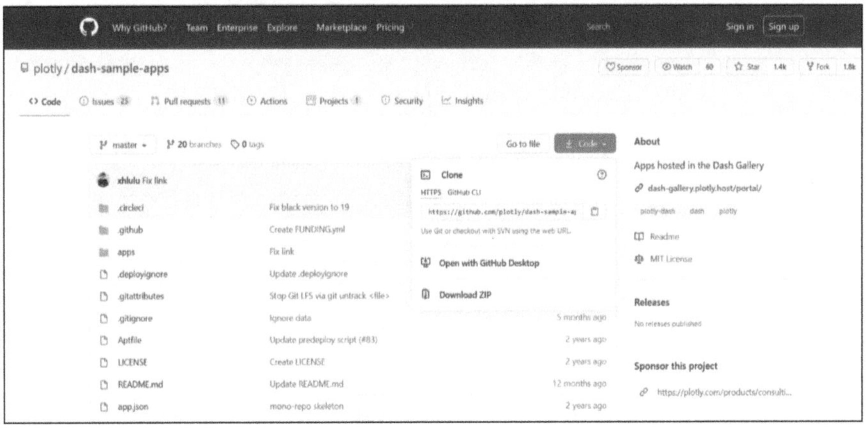

Figure 2-8: Sample Dash Gallery apps on GitHub

Click **Code** in the repository and copy the URL. For example, you can use *https://github.com/plotly/dash-sample-apps.git* to access a repository of all Dash apps from the gallery.

Open PyCharm and click **VCS ▶ Get from Version Control**, shown in Figure 2-9. Enter the URL in the URL field. Note that building this project will create a new project from the Git project URL, so it doesn't matter from which project you start.

Figure 2-9: Opening a GitHub repository in PyCharm

Click **Clone** and wait for the operation to finish. This may take some time because the repository contains all Dash Gallery projects. Installing the whole repository allows you to quickly try out many different Dash projects and examine how the experts implement the Dash features you're interested in.

Next, PyCharm asks you to set up a virtual environment to install the libraries the sample apps need (see Figure 2-10). Click **OK**. For troubleshooting, please follow the detailed strategy outlined at *https://www.jetbrains.com/help/pycharm/creating-virtual-environment.html*.

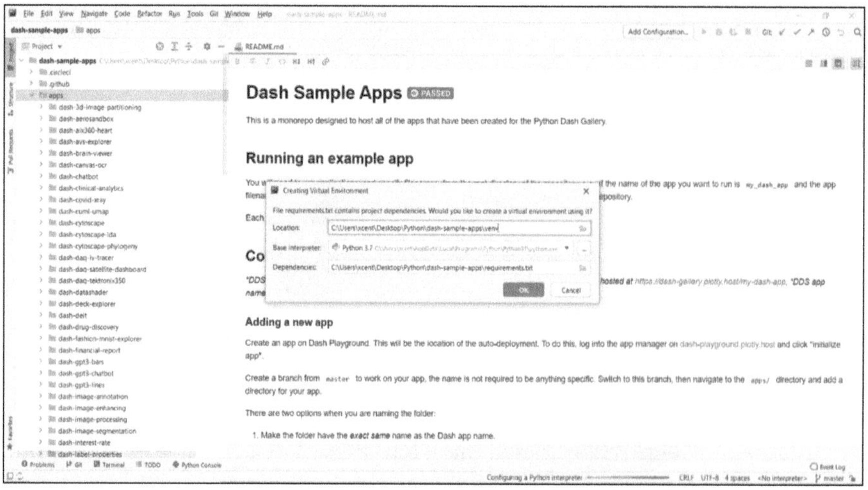

Figure 2-10: Installing libraries in a virtual environment for a checked-out GitHub repository in PyCharm

Congratulations! Your PyCharm project should now work. You've created a clone of the original GitHub project. A *clone* is simply a copy of the original project, so if you change the code in your clone, nobody but you can see the changes.

Figure 2-11 shows how you can open an individual dashboard app's main entry point: the file *app.py*. Open the file in PyCharm, install any dependencies it relies on, run it, and view it in your own browser.

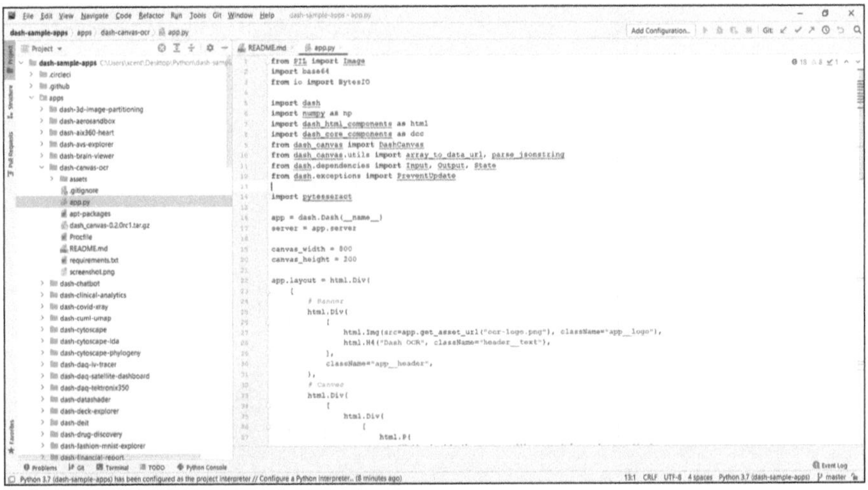

Figure 2-11: Opening the app.py file of a dashboard app from the Dash Gallery

If you'd like to see more example Dash apps, the Dash Gallery at *https://dash.gallery/Portal* points to many GitHub repositories created by Dash experts. Cloning them is as simple as replicating these steps using the URLs provided by the Dash Gallery. If you're not using PyCharm, you can check out this guide on how to clone an existing repository: *https://docs.github.com/en/github/creating-cloning-and-archiving-repositories/cloning-a-repository*. And don't worry—you cannot destroy anything, so feel free to play with the code. A version control system such as Git allows you to go back to the initial state easily.

Summary

In this chapter, you learned how to set up PyCharm, one of the most popular Python IDEs. PyCharm integrates well with Python Dash. Specifically, you learned how to install PyCharm and third-party libraries like Dash through PyCharm, create a first simple Dash project, run the project, and view your dashboard app in the browser. Furthermore, you learned how to integrate PyCharm with the most popular version control system, Git, so that you can check out existing Dash apps to learn and collaborate with others.

In fact, now would be a great time to follow the steps in this tutorial, clone one of the existing dashboard apps in the gallery, run it, and tweak simple things like colors and text labels to get accustomed to Dash! We'll explain everything in detail in the upcoming chapters, but it doesn't hurt to open the knowledge gap before trying to close it, does it?

With PyCharm installed, we'll move on to an introduction of the pandas library. The pandas library helps you organize and process the data you want to visualize in your dashboard app!

3

A CRASH COURSE IN PANDAS

Dashboard apps are mainly used to visualize data. But before you can do this, you need to preprocess, clean, and analyze the data. To help you accomplish this, Python provides a powerful suite of data analysis modules, including the popular pandas library. The *pandas library* provides data structures and functionality used to represent and manipulate data. Think of it like an advanced spreadsheet program in your code with extra functionality, including creating spreadsheets, accessing individual rows by name, calculating basic statistics, operating on cells that fulfill a certain condition, and much more.

This chapter provides a quick introduction to the most important pandas features. It is loosely based on the official "10 Minutes to pandas" guide, but here we compress the content to the most relevant information for this book. An eight-minute video tutorial for a pandas crash course can be found at *https://blog.finxter.com/pandas-quickstart*.

Visual Overview Cheat Sheet

Figure 3-1 gives a graphical overview of the topics described in this chapter.

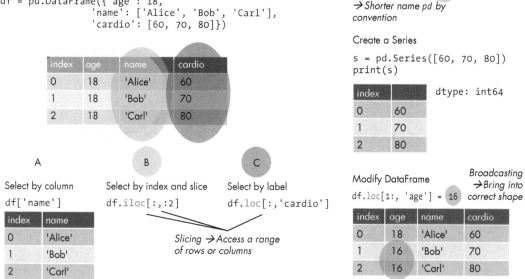

Figure 3-1: A pandas cheat sheet

Feel free to revisit this graphic as you read over this chapter. Let's dive into the detailed, step-by-step explanations in the following sections.

Installing pandas

Install the pandas library in your virtual environment or system using the following command in your terminal, command line, or shell:

```
$ pip install pandas
```

If you already have pandas installed, we recommend updating to the latest version with the command `pip install -U pandas`.

Some editors and IDEs have an integrated terminal that you can use to install pandas, including PyCharm, as shown in Figure 3-2. If you're using a different IDE, you can use either the terminal it provides or your operating system's terminal. If you have PyCharm installed, you can enter `import pandas` in the main editor and a tool tip should show. When you click the tool tip, it will give you the option of installing pandas, as shown in Figure 3-2.

Both ways to install pandas are displayed in Figure 3-2.

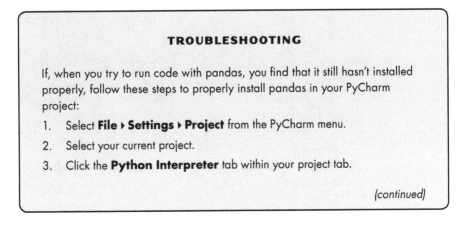

Figure 3-2: Install pandas in PyCharm using either the tool tips (1) or the integrated terminal, with the command `pip install pandas` (2).

To access the pandas library in your Python scripts, you simply import it with the `import pandas` statement. It's common to give pandas the alias `pd` for ease of access and brevity, so the full line to add to the top of your script would be:

```
import pandas as pd
```

With this, instead of `pandas.somefunction()`, you can now call `pd.somefunction()`.

TROUBLESHOOTING

If, when you try to run code with pandas, you find that it still hasn't installed properly, follow these steps to properly install pandas in your PyCharm project:

1. Select **File ▶ Settings ▶ Project** from the PyCharm menu.
2. Select your current project.
3. Click the **Python Interpreter** tab within your project tab.

(continued)

---

4. Click the small plus symbol (+) to add a new library to the project.

5. Enter the name of the library to be installed, which here is **pandas**, and click **Install Package**.

6. Wait for the installation to terminate, and then close all pop-up windows.

Creating Objects in pandas

The two most important data types in pandas are Series and DataFrames. A pandas Series is a one-dimensional array of data values, like a column in an Excel sheet. A pandas DataFrame is a two-dimensional labeled data structure, much like a full spreadsheet. The purpose of the Series and DataFrame structures is to facilitate data storage, access, and analysis.

In order to provide easy access to individual rows or columns using indexing, pandas automatically adds row and column indices to DataFrame structures when you create them. By default, pandas uses zero-based indexing, so it starts at index 0 and increments the subsequent index by one until it reaches the end of the data structure.

Series

To follow along with the pandas examples in your PyCharm IDE, create a new project by selecting **File ▸ New Project**, and then create a new empty Python file with **File ▸ New ▸ Python File**. You can assign any name you want to both the project and the Python file. In the new project file, copy the following code for creating a simple Series object (make sure you've installed pandas):

```
import pandas as pd

s = pd.Series([42, 21, 7, 3.5])
print(s)
```

Run the code and you should see the following:

```
0    42.0
1    21.0
2     7.0
3     3.5
dtype: float64
```

You've just created a Series with the pd.Series() constructor, passing it a list of values. You can also create a Series from other data types by passing, for example, a list of integers, a tuple of Booleans, or any other iterable of data values, for that matter, and pandas will automatically determine the data type of the whole series and assign it to the Series object, as shown in the last line of the output.

DataFrames

A pandas DataFrame is like a data table in your code, with rows, columns, and cells filled with data of a certain type, as depicted in Figure 3-3.

Create a DataFrame

```
df = pd.DataFrame({'age': 18,
                   'name': ['Alice', 'Bob', 'Carl'],
                   'cardio': [60, 70, 80]})
```

index	age	name	cardio
0	18	'Alice'	60
1	18	'Bob'	70
2	18	'Carl'	80

Figure 3-3: Creating a pandas DataFrame object with three columns (excluding the index column) and three rows

Listing 3-1 shows how to create a simple DataFrame object.

```
import pandas as pd
df = pd.DataFrame({'age': 18,
                   'name': ['Alice', 'Bob', 'Carl'],
                   'cardio': [60, 70, 80]})
print(df)
```

Listing 3-1: The example DataFrame named df

This will give us a DataFrame that looks like this:

```
   age   name   cardio
0  18    Alice  60
1  18    Bob    70
2  18    Carl   80
```

You create the DataFrame with the pd.DataFrame() constructor. When you use a dictionary to initialize a DataFrame, as we did here, the dictionary keys are the column names and the dictionary values are the row values for that column. You can also provide just one column value, such as 18, and assign it to a whole column name, such as age, so that every cell in that column is filled with the value 18.

NOTE *Technically, if only a single value is provided for all the rows of a specific column, pandas will automatically set the same value to all existing rows in the DataFrame, a process known as broadcasting.*

DataFrames can also be constructed by reading data from a CSV file. You use the pandas read_csv() function to load the CSV file as a DataFrame, like so:

```
import pandas as pd

path = "your/path/to/CSV/file.csv"
df = pd.read_csv(path)
```

You'll need to replace the path to the file with your specific filepath; this can be an absolute path or a relative path from the location where your script resides. For instance, if the CSV file is in the same directory as your Python script, you can simply give the filename as a relative path.

Selecting Elements in DataFrames

Series objects and DataFrames allow for easy access to individual elements. Here we'll see how to store, access, and analyze data from DataFrames in a simple, efficient, and readable manner. Series objects can be seen as just one-dimensional DataFrames, so understanding DataFrame access will explain Series access too. Figure 3-4 shows the relevant sections of the cheat sheet for your convenience. You can see there are three ways to access data: select by column (A), select by index and slice (B), and select by label (C). The following subsections provide a brief overview of each. We'll dive into more detail in subsequent chapters.

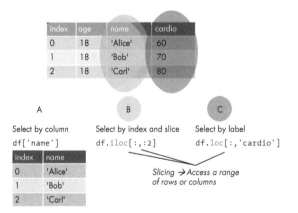

Figure 3-4: Three different ways to select elements in a DataFrame

Select by Column

You can access a column with the square bracket notation you already know from Python lists and dictionaries. Using the df DataFrame from Listing 3-1, we select all elements in the age column, like so:

```
print(df['age'])
```

This will print:

```
0    18
1    18
2    18
Name: age, dtype: int64
```

You select all values in the column labeled age using the name of the DataFrame you're accessing and the column name in square brackets.

Note that pandas allows the alternative syntax df.age for accessing columns. While you will see this in some pandas code bases, the more popular way is to use the square bracket notation df['age'], like for standard Python list, string, and dictionary indexing.

Select by Index and Slice

To access specific rows in the DataFrame, we use the slicing notation df[start:stop]. As mentioned in Chapter 1, the row with the start index is included and the row with the stop index is excluded from the selection. Be careful when using df.loc[start:stop], however: the stop index is actually *included*, and is a common source of confusion!

NOTE *You can find comprehensive tutorials about slicing in Python at* https://blog.finxter .com/introduction-to-slicing-in-python *and slicing in NumPy at* https://blog .finxter.com/numpy-tutorial.

To access only one row, set the start and stop indices accordingly:

```
print(df[2:3])
```

This will print the row at index 2 and, by specifying a stop index of 3, will print no further lines:

```
   age   name   cardio
2   18   Carl   80
```

You can also access DataFrame elements using the iloc index to access the i-th row and the j-th column. Here we access the third row and the second column in the df DataFrame with zero-based indices 2 and 1, respectively:

```
print(df.iloc[2, 1])
```

The first argument i accesses the i-th row and the second argument j accesses the j-th column of the iloc index. This will print the data value in the third row (with index 2) and the second column (with index 1), which 'Carl'.

Boolean Indexing

A powerful way to access rows that match a certain condition is with *Boolean indexing*. We'll again use our df DataFrame and access the rows with a value larger than 60 in the `cardio` column (stay with us for a moment; we'll explain this shortly):

```
print(df[df['cardio']>60])
```

This will extract the last two rows:

```
    age   name   cardio
1   18    Bob    70
2   18    Carl   80
```

While this syntax may appear strange at first, it is actually well designed by the pandas creators. The inner condition `df['cardio']>60` results in a Series of Boolean values that are `'True'` if the i-th element of the `cardio` column is larger than 60. This holds for the last two rows of the DataFrame. Thus, `df['cardio']>60` results in the Series:

```
0    False
1    True
2    True
Name: Cardio, dtype: bool
```

These Boolean values are then passed as indices into the `df` DataFrame, which results in a DataFrame with only two rows instead of three.

Select by Label

Like in spreadsheets, each row and each column in pandas is labeled. The label can be either an integer index number, such as the row indices, or a string name, such as the `cardio` column name in the `df` DataFrame. To access data by label, we use the indexing mechanism `df.loc[rows, columns]`. Here we access all rows of the `name` column of the `df` DataFrame:

```
print(df.loc[:, 'name'])
```

This gives us:

```
0    Alice
1      Bob
2     Carl
Name: name, dtype: object
'''
```

We use the comma-separated slicing indexing scheme within the square brackets `df.loc[:, 'name']`, where the first part, `:`, selects the rows and the second part, `'name'`, selects the columns to be retrieved from the DataFrame. The empty slice colon, without specified start and stop indices, indicates that you want to access all rows without restriction. The string `'name'` indicates that you want to retrieve only the values from the column `name` and ignore the rest.

To access all rows from the columns age and cardio, we'd pass a list of column labels, like so:

```
print(df.loc[:, ['age', 'cardio']])
```

And this results in:

	age	cardio
0	18	60
1	18	70
2	18	80

Modifying an Existing DataFrame

You can modify and even overwrite a part of your DataFrame using the assignment operator = by selecting the data to be replaced on the left and providing the new data on the right. Here we overwrite all the integer values in the age column to 16:

```
df['age'] = 16
print(s)
```

Here is the result:

	age	name	cardio
0	16	Alice	60
1	16	Bob	70
2	16	Carl	80

You first select the age column with df['age'] and overwrite the value associated with age with the integer value 16. To copy the single integer to all rows in the column, pandas uses broadcasting.

Figure 3-5 shows the relevant part of the pandas cheat sheet.

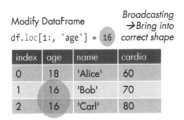

Figure 3-5: Modifying rows 2 and 3 of column age in the DataFrame using slicing and broadcasting

Here's a more advanced example that uses slicing and the loc index to overwrite all but the first row of the age column. First we'll rebuild the original df DataFrame:

```
import pandas as pd


df = pd.DataFrame({'age': 18,
                   'name': ['Alice', 'Bob', 'Carl'],
                   'cardio': [60, 70, 80]})
```

This gives us:

```
   age   name   cardio
0  18    Alice  60
1  18    Bob    70
2  18    Carl   80
```

Now we exclude the first row from the changes by selecting the second and third rows using the standard slicing notation:

```
df.loc[1:,'age'] = 16
print(df)
```

We can see Alice's age remains 18:

```
   age   name   cardio
0  18    Alice  60
1  16    Bob    70
2  16    Carl   80
```

To add variety to our examples, we'll use a new system, as pandas is very flexible. By understanding the different indexing schemes—bracket notation, slicing, loc, and iloc—you'll be able to overwrite existing data and add new data. Here we add a new column, friend, with the loc index, slicing, and broadcasting:

```
df.loc[:,'friend'] = 'Alice'
print(df)
```

This gives us:

```
   age   name   cardio  friend
0  18    Alice  60      Alice
1  16    Bob    70      Alice
2  16    Carl   80      Alice
```

Note that the same can be achieved with the simpler code shown here:

```
df['friend'] = 'Alice'
print(df)
```

And we get the same result:

	age	name	cardio	friend
0	18	Alice	60	Alice
1	16	Bob	70	Alice
2	16	Carl	80	Alice

Summary

This was a quick crash course on the most relevant features of pandas that we'll use in the book. The pandas library has many more functionalities, including calculating statistics, plotting, grouping, and reshaping, to name just a few. We recommend exploring pandas at your leisure using the links in this chapter's Resources section. Once you understand the concepts discussed in this chapter, you'll be able to read and understand existing pandas code in many other Dash projects.

Now, let's get started with your first dashboard app!

Resources

- "10 Minutes to pandas": *https://pandas.pydata.org/pandas-docs/stable/user_guide/10min.html*
- *Coffee Break Pandas*, a free ebook available at this book's companion website, *https://learnplotlydash.com*

PART II

BUILDING APPLICATIONS

Part II will walk you through four separate applications as we teach you how to utilize the most common components and go over the most important concepts of Dash. You will also learn about several popular graphs from the Plotly graphing library as we explain how to visualize a variety of datasets. You will create an app that analyzes social media data, an app that retrieves data in real time, an app that explores how asset allocation affects the returns of an investment portfolio, and an app that visualizes machine learning models. At the end, we will provide you with tips and tricks that will make learning Dash and building your own apps even easier and more enjoyable.

4

FIRST DASH APP

In this chapter you'll build your first Dash app. We'll analyze the number of Twitter likes received by 16 chosen celebrities since 2011. You can download the data with the book's resources at *https://nostarch.com/python-dash*. The type of analysis we'll do is common in the field of social media analytics, typically used to better understand audience behavior, the effectiveness of posts, and the overall performance of an account.

This first dashboard will plot the number of likes per tweet. Once you master this simple plotting process with Dash, you'll be able to scale your skills to plot bigger and more complex data in other areas: Instagram post views, Facebook profile visits, LinkedIn post click-through rates, and YouTube video performance.

This chapter should give you sufficient knowledge of Dash to create your own dashboard app. You'll learn how to incorporate data into your app, manage numerous dashboard app components, build basic charts such as line charts, and add interactive capabilities to your dashboard through the callback decorator. First, let's download the code and run the app to see what it does.

Setting Up the Project

Open PyCharm, create a new project, and call it *my-first-app* (the project name should be the suffix text after the last backslash in the Location field of the New Project dialog). Set up your virtual environment using the standard Virtualenv.

NOTE *The code in this chapter assumes you're using a Python IDE, such as PyCharm. If you don't have an IDE installed and a virtual environment set, refer back to Chapter 2 and complete your Python setup. If you're using a different coding environment, just adapt the instructions here to your environment. The code in this chapter also requires Python 3.6 or higher.*

Next, you need to download this chapter's dashboard app files into your project folder. Instead of cloning the repository as we did in Chapter 2, we'll download the ZIP file directly. It's worth trying various ways to set up a project because you'll probably stumble upon some projects that are not directly available as Git repositories. To use the ZIP file, go to the GitHub repository at *https://github.com/DashBookProject/Plotly-Dash*, click **Code**, and then click **Download ZIP**, as shown in Figure 4-1.

Figure 4-1: Downloading the app code from GitHub

Once you have the *Plotly-Dash-master.zip* file on your computer, open it and go into the *Chapter-4* folder. Copy all the files from that folder into your recently created *my-first-app* project folder. The project folder should have files in the following structure:

```
- my-first-app
|--assets
    --mystyles.css
|--tweets.csv
|--twitter_app.py
```

The *assets* folder will hold the CSS script. The *tweets.csv* file holds the data we'll use, and *twitter_app.py* is the main app file we'll use to run the app.

We'll now install the necessary libraries in our virtual environment. Go to the Terminal tab in the bottom part of the PyCharm window, shown in Figure 4-2.

Figure 4-2: Opening the terminal in PyCharm

Enter and execute the following lines of code to install pandas and Dash (the Plotly package is automatically installed with Dash, so there is no need to install Plotly, and the NumPy package is automatically installed with pandas):

```
$ pip install pandas
$ pip install dash
```

To check that the libraries are installed correctly, enter:

```
$ pip list
```

This will create a list of all the Python packages currently in your virtual environment. If they're all listed, you can move on. Note that all dependencies of pandas and Dash will also be listed, so you might see many more libraries than just the two you installed.

Next, open *twitter_app.py* inside PyCharm and run the script. You should see the following message:

```
* Serving Flask app "twitter_app" (lazy loading)
* Environment: production
WARNING: This is a development server. Do not use it in a production deployment.
Use a production WSGI server instead.
* Debug mode: on
Dash is running on http://127.0.0.1:8050/
```

The warning just reminds us that the app is in a development server and it is completely normal. To open your app, click the HTTP link or copy and paste it into your browser's address bar.

Congratulations! You should now see your first Dash app, which should look like Figure 4-3.

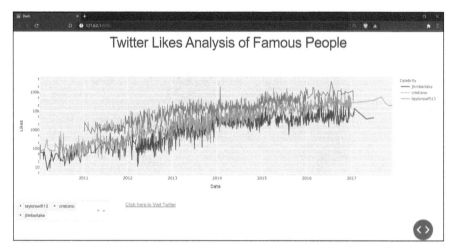

Figure 4-3: The Twitter Likes Analysis app

Have fun! Play around with your dashboard app. Change the dropdown values, click the links, click on the graph legend, and zoom in to a certain date range by holding down the mouse's left-click button and dragging the mouse. See what information you can deduce.

Now let's take a look at the code of the app. Most Dash apps have a similar code layout:

1. Import the necessary Python libraries.
2. Read in the data.
3. Assign a stylesheet to describe how the app should be displayed.
4. Build the app layout that will define how to display all the elements.
5. Create the callbacks to enable interactivity between the app components.

Because Dash apps mostly follow this outline, we'll go through the code in this order.

Importing the Libraries

Let's first look at the libraries we'll use, shown in Listing 4-1.

```
import pandas as pd
import plotly.express as px
from dash import Dash, dcc, html, Input, Output
```

Listing 4-1: The import section of twitter_app.py

We first import pandas to handle the data. We then import Plotly, a popular Python visualization library. There are two main ways to create graphs in Plotly. We're using *Plotly Express*, a high-level interface for creating graphs in single function calls, with very few lines of code. It has enough features to allow you to build graphs seamlessly and quickly, and is the easier of the two to use for simpler apps.

The alternative is *Plotly Graph Objects*, a low-level interface for creating graphs from the bottom up. When using Graph Objects, you need to define the data, layout, and, at times, frames, all of which make the graph-building process more involved. That said, its full set of features allows you to customize your graphs in ways that add much richness to them, so you might want to use Plotly Graph Objects once you've mastered Dash basics and you have more complicated graphs to build. We'll use Plotly Express in most cases and revert to Graph Objects in more complex situations.

Next, we import some Dash libraries to handle components and dependencies. *Components* are the building blocks that can be combined to create rich, complex interfaces for your users, such as dropdown menus, range sliders, and radio buttons. Dash comes bundled with two key component libraries maintained by Plotly: dash-html-components (HTML) and dash-core-components (DCC). The *dash-html-components* library contains structural elements such as headings and dividers that style and position elements on the page, while *dash-core-components* provides core functionality for your app, such as user input fields and figures.

Data Management

In this app, we're using a CSV spreadsheet as our data source. To use the data, we need to read it into memory via pandas, but before that we have to *clean* the data. This means preparing the data for analysis and plotting by doing things like standardizing capitalization of strings and formats of time, stripping whitespace, and adding nulls for missing values. When the data is *dirty*, it's often unorganized and might contain missing values. If you try to use dirty data, the plot may not work, the analysis is likely to be inaccurate, and you'll find filtering difficult. Cleaning the data ensures that it is readable, presentable, and plottable.

Listing 4-2 shows the data management section of the code.

```
❶ df = pd.read_csv("tweets.csv")
df["name"] = pd.Series(df["name"]).str.lower()
df["date_time"] = pd.to_datetime(df["date_time"])
df = (
    df.groupby([df["date_time"].dt.date, "name"])[
        ["number_of_likes", "number_of_shares"]
    ]
    .mean()
    .astype(int)
)
df = df.reset_index()
```

Listing 4-2: The data management section of twitter_app.py

At ❶ we take the CSV spreadsheet and read it into a pandas DataFrame called df. The DataFrame at the beginning of a Dash app is commonly referred to as a *global DataFrame* and the data is a *global variable* (*global* means the object is declared outside a function, meaning it's accessible throughout the app).

To clean the data, we change the strings of the celebrity name column to lowercase so that we can readily compare them, we convert the date_time column into a date recognizable by pandas, and we group the data by date _time and name so that each row has a unique date stamp and name. If we did not group the data this way, we would end up with multiple rows with the same date and name, which would create a messy line chart that's impossible to read.

To check the data, add the following line of code to the script, right after df = df.reset_index():

```
print(df.head())
```

Once you run the script anew, you should see something like the following inside the Python terminal:

	date_time	name	number_of_likes	number_of_shares
0	2010-01-06	selenagomez	278	695
1	2010-01-07	jtimberlake	62	189
2	2010-01-07	selenagomez	201	630
3	2010-01-08	jtimberlake	27	107
4	2010-01-08	selenagomez	349	935

As you can see, the result is a neat pandas DataFrame with rows of data that represent the average number of likes and shares per celebrity, per day.

It's always a good practice to read in and prepare your data at the beginning of the app because reading data can be a memory-expensive task; by inserting the data at the beginning, you ensure that the app loads the data into memory only once and does not repeat this process every time a user interacts with the dashboard.

Layout and Styling

The next step is to manage the layout and styling of the app components, such as the title, graph, and dropdown menus. We'll learn more about the components in "Dash Components" later in this chapter; here we'll just focus on the layout section.

In a Dash app, the *layout* refers to the alignment of the components within the app. The *style* refers to how the elements look, such as the color, size, spacing, and other properties (known in Dash as *props*). Styling the app allows for a more customized, professional presentation. Without styling, you could end up with an app like the one shown in Figure 4-4, where the title is not centered, the dropdown field stretches over the whole page, and there is no space between the link and the dropdown above it.

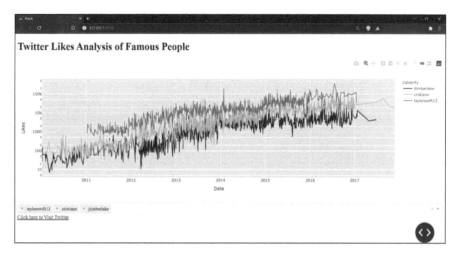

Figure 4-4: The Twitter Likes Analysis app without proper layout and styling

Alignment

Dash apps are web-based, so they use the standard language of web pages: HTML (HyperText Markup Language). Luckily, Dash includes the Dash HTML Components module, which converts Python to HTML, meaning we can use Python to write our HTML.

One of the most essential components of HTML is the Div, short for *division*, which is simply a container for other elements and a way to group elements together. Every component we use in a Dash app will be contained inside a Div, and a Div can contain multiple components. We build the Div, then style it to tell the web browser exactly where to position it and how much space it should take up.

Say we're creating a dashboard app with three dropdown menus, represented by the keyword Dropdown, as in Listing 4-3.

```
app.layout = html.Div([
    html.Div(dcc.Dropdown()),
    html.Div(dcc.Dropdown()),
    html.Div(dcc.Dropdown()),
])
```

Listing 4-3: Example Div code (not part of the main app)

The line app.layout creates a layout for this Dash app. Everything related to the layout must be placed within app.layout. We then create a Div that contains three dropdown menus.

A Div by default will take up the full width of the parent container, meaning it's assumed to be one big cell that takes up the width of the page. As it is, the first Dropdown will appear in the top left and fill the whole page from left to right. The second Dropdown will appear right below the first Dropdown and fill the whole width of the page as well, and so on with the third Dropdown. In other words, each Div will take up the full width of the page and force neighboring elements onto a new line.

To best control how much space a `Div` is allocated, we should define the web page as a grid of rows and columns and place each `Div` within a specific cell inside that grid. We can quickly define rows and columns using a premade CSS stylesheet. CSS (Cascading Style Sheets) is another web language used to define how a page should be displayed. We put the stylesheet in an external file or call one from an online directory into our app. We're using a stylesheet from *https://codepen.io*. Written by Chris Parmer, the creator of Plotly Dash, the stylesheet is comprehensive and suitable to use for a basic Dash app. In Listing 4-4, we import the CSS. We also tell *twitter_app.py* to grab the CSS stylesheet from the web and incorporate it into the app, and we instantiate our app with `Dash`.

```
stylesheets = ['https://codepen.io/chriddyp/pen/bWLwgP.css']
app = Dash(__name__, external_stylesheets=stylesheets)
```

Listing 4-4: Importing a stylesheet into twitter_app.py

Our CSS stylesheet describes the width and height of the columns and rows on the page using CSS classes. We just need to refer to these classes within our Dash code to place the `Div` content in specific cells inside the grid.

First, we must assign the rows because the columns should be wrapped by rows. To do so, we set a string value `"row"` to the `className`. Let's build on the `Div` example in Listing 4-3, assuming this code has imported the custom stylesheet; the new code is in bold (see Listing 4-5).

```
app.layout = html.Div([
    html.Div(dcc.Dropdown()),
    html.Div(dcc.Dropdown()),
    html.Div(dcc.Dropdown()),
], className="row")
```

Listing 4-5: Example Div code with className *(not part of the main app)*

Here we assign one row to the `html.Div` that houses all three drop-downs, so all these dropdowns will be displayed in the same row on the page (Figure 4-5). `className` is a prop that can be assigned classes from a CSS stylesheet to tell Dash how to style an element. Here we assign it the `row` class, which tells the app that all the components inside this `Div` should be on the same row. Every Dash component will have a `className`, commonly used to style and define layouts. We use the `className` prop of `html.Div` to describe the row and column layout of each `Div`.

After defining the row, we need to define the columns' widths so that Dash knows how many columns of space to allocate to each component within that row. We do this for each `html.Div` contained in the row, as shown in bold in Listing 4-6.

```
app.layout = html.Div([
    html.Div(dcc.Dropdown(), className="four columns"),
    html.Div(dcc.Dropdown(), className="four columns"),
    html.Div(dcc.Dropdown(), className="four columns"),
], className="row")
```

Listing 4-6: Setting the column width (not part of the main app)

We set the number of columns of space each `Div` component should fill with a string value set to `className` and formatted like `"one column"` or `"two columns"` and so on. Most web pages will have a maximum of 12 columns (and a potentially unlimited number of rows), meaning the sum of the components' column widths must never surpass 12, so here we set them to fill 4 columns each. Note that we don't have to fill all 12 columns.

Figure 4-5 shows how this simple page would be displayed.

Figure 4-5: Demo of three dropdowns on one row

With all this in mind, let's have a look at Listing 4-7, the `html.Div` section of our *twitter_app.py* file, which has fewer than 12 columns.

```
html.Div(
    [
❶       html.Div(
            dcc.Dropdown(
                id="my-dropdown",
                multi=True,
                options=[
                    {"label": x, "value": x}
                    for x in sorted(df["name"].unique())
                ],
                value=["taylorswift13", "cristiano", "jtimberlake"],
            ),
            className="three columns",
        ),
❷       html.Div(
            html.A(
                id="my-link",
                children="Click here to Visit Twitter",
                href="https://twitter.com/explore",
                target="_blank",
            ),
            className="two columns",
        ),
    ],
    className="row",
),
```

Listing 4-7: The Dropdown section of twitter_app.py

We see that the row contains two `Div`s: a `Dropdown` that offers multiple celebrities to choose from ❶ and a link for the user to click ❷. Those two `Div`s have the sum of just five columns, meaning they're left-aligned on the page, as shown in Figure 4-6.

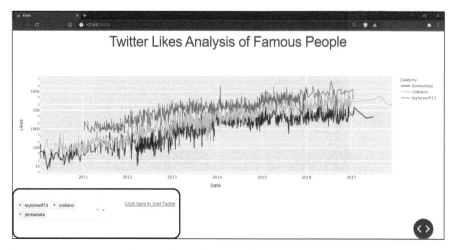

Figure 4-6: Components that are five columns wide

Note that some stylesheets, including the one we're working with here, require us to create the parent `Div` first and assign a row to it. Then, within the children of the parent `Div`, we define the column width of each inner `Div`.

Styling: Embellishing Your App

The styling is what gives life to the app. We can add color, change the font and size of the text, underline text, and much more. There are two main ways to alter the style of the app. The first is to use the `style` prop inside the Dash HTML component. This allows the user to specify CSS styling declarations that will be applied directly to the component.

The second method is to refer to a CSS stylesheet, like we did to create rows and columns. We'll show you how to integrate the additional stylesheet *mystyles.css* into the app; if you downloaded the files as described in "Setting Up the Project" earlier in this chapter, this should be in your *assets* folder. Let's first look at how to use the `style` prop to alter the app.

Using the style Prop

The style prop expects a Python dictionary, with keys that specify what aspect we want to alter and values that set the style. In our *twitter_app.py* file, we'll change the text color of the link to red by defining the `style` prop within the `html.A` component used for adding URL links, as shown in Listing 4-8.

```
html.Div(
    html.A(id="my-link", children="Click here to Visit Twitter",
        href="https://twitter.com/explore", target="_blank",
❶ style={"color": "red"}),
    className="two columns")
```

Listing 4-8: Styling HTML elements of twitter_app.py

At ❶ we assign a dictionary to the style prop, where the key is color and the value is red. This tells the browser to render this link with red text.

Now we'll add a yellow background color to the same link by adding another key-value pair to the dictionary:

```
style={"color": "red", "backgroundColor": "yellow"}
```

Notice that the dictionary key is a camelCased string. In Dash, the keys in the style dictionary should always be camelCased.

Lastly, we'll change the link's font size to 40 pixels:

```
style={"color": "red", "backgroundColor": "yellow", "fontSize": "40px"}
```

A beautiful thing about Dash is that styling is not limited to HTML components; we can also style the Core components, such as the Dropdown. For example, to change the text color of the dropdown options to green, we add the style prop within dcc.Dropdown, as shown in Listing 4-9.

```
html.Div(
    dcc.Dropdown(id="my-dropdown", multi=True,
            options=[{"label": x, "value": x}
                    for x in sorted(df["name"].unique())],
            value=["taylorswift13", "cristiano", "jtimberlake"],
            style={"color": "green"}),
    className="three columns"),
```

Listing 4-9: Styling Core components in twitter_app.py

The dropdown options shown in the bottom-left corner of Figure 4-7 will now be green instead of black.

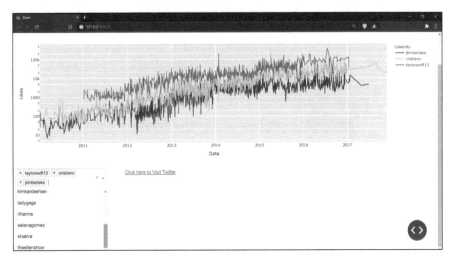

Figure 4-7: Dropdown options that appear in green when run on your computer

Using a Stylesheet

The second way to style app components is to define styles through elements or classes. Typically, we use this method when a lot of code is needed for the styling. To reduce the amount of code present in the app itself, we use styling code in an external CSS stylesheet. CSS stylesheets are also reusable; you can define a particular class once and apply it to multiple components.

The CSS stylesheet we'll use is *mystyles.css*, and it should already be in the *assets* folder you downloaded with the book's resources. Open the CSS stylesheet inside PyCharm or your preferred text editor by double-clicking it, and you should see these lines of code:

```
/*
h1 { font-size: 8.6rem; line-height: 1.35; letter-spacing: -.08rem;
margin-bottom: 1.2rem; margin-top: 1.2rem;}
*/
```

The /* is comment syntax, so to enable the styling, delete the /* and */ symbols below and above the CSS code. Here h1 is the *selector*, which specifies the element we want to apply the subsequent styles to; in this case, it's all h1 elements. Inside the curly brackets we declare properties and property values that will set various styles inside the app. In this example, we set the element's font size to 8.6, the line height to 1.35, the spacing between letters to −0.08, and the top and bottom margins to 1.2.

Listing 4-10 shows how the H1 heading component in our app uses this CSS stylesheet.

```
html.Div(html.H1("Twitter Likes Analysis of Famous People",
            style={"textAlign": "center"}),
        className="row"),
```

Listing 4-10: The html.H1 component in twitter_app.py

The html.H1 through html.H6 components are used to define headings, with H1 representing the highest heading level and H6 representing the lowest heading level. Figure 4-8 shows how this header styling should look.

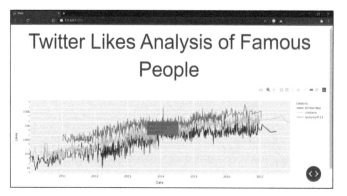

Figure 4-8: App title styled with CSS

As you can see if you compare Figure 4-8 to Figure 4-6, the result is a much larger font size for the app's title, with more top and bottom margin space around the title and less space between the letters. If your app's title did not change in size, restart your app to see the result.

If you'd like to revert back to a smaller font size for the title, simply comment out the CSS code by reinserting the /* and */ symbols, as such:

```
/*
h1 { font-size: 8.6rem; line-height: 1.35; letter-spacing: -.08rem;
margin-bottom: 1.2rem; margin-top: 1.2rem;}
*/
```

You have learned how to manipulate the style and layout of your app with pure Python. This is just the beginning, though. In Chapter 5, we will dive into dash-bootstrap-components, which will make the layout design and styling of the dashboard app even easier and more varied.

Dash Components

Here we'll provide an overview of some common components in Dash, provided by the dash-html-components and dash-core-components libraries. There are many other component libraries, and you can even write your own! But dash-html-components and dash-core-components contain most of the basic functionality we need. The HTML components are generally for composing the layout of the web page and include Div, Button, H1, and Form, among many others. The Core components—such as Dropdown, Checklist, RangeSlider, and many more—are for creating an interactive experience. All HTML and Core components have props that add to their functionality. For a full list of these props and their components, visit the Dash documentation on HTML and Core components at *https://dash.plotly.com/dash-core-components*.

HTML Components

Dash HTML components are written in Python and are automatically converted to HTML, so there's no need to become an expert on HTML or CSS to use Dash apps. The following line of code in Python

```
<h1> Twitter Likes Analysis of Famous People </h1>
```

is roughly equivalent to the following line of HTML that is read by a web browser:

```
html.H1("Twitter Likes Analysis of Famous People")
```

Writing a complete dashboard app is now possible in pure Python: Python forever!

To create an HTML component, you use dot notation between the html keyword and the component name. For example, for a Div component you would use html.Div, as we saw earlier. We also saw two additional

HTML components: html.H1, which creates a top-level heading, and html.A, which creates a hyperlink. Let's take a closer look at the use of html.H1 to represent the title of the page, with the title itself written as a string, like so:

```
html.H1("Twitter Likes Analysis of Famous People")
```

This assigns the string to the children prop, which is usually the first positional argument of any component that accepts children. children, in this context, is a prop that places a component or element (like a text label) within another component. Written in full, the previous line looks like this:

```
html.H1(children="Twitter Likes Analysis of Famous People")
```

In the first three examples of the following code, the children prop adds text to the page. In the last example, with html.Div, the children prop adds the html.H1 component to the page, which has text as well. The children prop can take an integer, a string, a Dash component, or a list of any of these. All these examples are possible:

```
html.H1(children=2),
html.H1(children="Twitter Likes Analysis of Famous People"),
html.H1(children=["Twitter Likes Analysis of Famous People"]),
html.Div(children=[
    html.H1("Twitter Likes Analysis of Famous People"),
    html.H2("Twitter Likes Analysis of Famous People")
])
```

The html.A component creates an <a> HTML5 element, which is used to create hyperlinks. In this component, shown in Listing 4-11, we use four props: id, children, href, and target.

```
html.A(id="my-link", children="Click here to Visit Twitter",
    href="https://twitter.com/explore", target="_blank")
```

Listing 4-11: The HTML link component in twitter_app.py

The value we assign to href is the full link destination, where the user will end up after clicking the link. The target prop indicates where the link will open: if its assigned value is _self, the link will open in the same tab of the browser the user is in; if its assigned value is _blank, the link will open in a new browser tab. The children prop defines the content of the component, which here is a string value representing the link's text that the user sees on the page.

The id prop is important because Dash components use id to identify and interact with each other, which gives the dashboard app its interactive capabilities. We'll go over this in more detail in "Callback Decorator" later in this chapter. For now, just note that the value assigned to id must be a unique string so that it can be used to identify the component.

Core Components

The Dash Core components are prebuilt components from the Dash library that allow the user to interact with the app in an intuitive way. In this app we use two Core components: Graph and Dropdown. To build or access a particular Core component, we use the dcc keyword and the dot notation before the component name, such as dcc.Dropdown.

The Graph Component

The Graph component allows you to incorporate data visualizations into your app in the form of plots, charts, and graphs written with Plotly. It's one of the most popular of the Core components, and you'll likely see it in every analytic dashboard app.

A Graph component has two main props: id and figure. Here's the template for defining a Graph component:

```
dcc.Graph(id="line-chart", figure={})
```

The id prop gives the Graph component a unique ID. The figure prop is the placeholder for the Plotly chart. Once a Plotly chart is created, we would assign it to the figure prop in place of the empty dictionary. For example, in our app we create a Plotly line chart with the line shown in Listing 4-12.

```
import plotly.express as px

--snip--

fig = px.line(data_frame=df_filtered, x="date_time", y="number_of_likes",
    color="name", log_y=True)
```

Listing 4-12: Creating a Plotly chart in twitter_app.py

We'll go through Plotly charts in "Plotly Express Line Charts" later in this chapter. For now, this line simply describes how the chart should look and assigns it to the fig object, making it a Plotly figure. We can then insert fig into dcc.Graph's figure prop to display the line chart on the page. Listing 4-13 shows the code from the *twitter_app.py* file that does just that, assigned to app.layout.

```
html.Div(dcc.Graph(id="line-chart", figure=fig), className="row")
```

Listing 4-13: Pulling the chart into the Graph component in twitter_app.py

We put the Graph component inside the Div component and assign it to a single row on the page. Once the complete app script is activated, the line chart should display on the page.

For a complete video tutorial on the Dash Graph component and its usage, see the video "All About the Graph Component" at *https://learnplotly dash.com*.

The Dropdown Component

The Dropdown component allows users to choose options from a dropdown menu to dynamically filter data and update graphs. We define the Dropdown component by providing values for four props: id, multi, options, and value, as shown in Listing 4-14. This menu is shown in Figure 4-9.

```
dcc.Dropdown(id="my-dropdown", multi=True,
             options=[{"label": x, "value": x}
                 for x in sorted(df["name"].unique())],
             value=["taylorswift13", "cristiano", "jtimberlake"])
```

Listing 4-14: Creating a Dropdown component in twitter_app.py

The multi prop allows us to choose whether the user can select multiple values at once or just one value at a time. When this prop is set to True, the app user can select multiple values. When it's set to False, the app user can select only one value at a time.

The options prop represents the values the user can choose from when they click the Dropdown. We assign it a list of dictionaries of label and value keys, where each dictionary represents one menu option. The label is the name the user sees as the option, and the value is the actual data read by the app.

Figure 4-9: App dropdown options

In Listing 4-14, we assigned the list of dictionaries using list comprehension, a Python shortcut that creates a new list based on values of another list (or any other Python iterable). For every unique value in the name column of our pandas DataFrame, this line creates a dictionary of label and value keys.

If instead we only have a few values, it may be easier to write out each dictionary instead of using list comprehension. For example, in Listing 4-15 we build a Dropdown with only two values: taylorswift13 and cristiano.

```
dcc.Dropdown(id="my-dropdown", multi=True,
            options=[{"label": "Taylor", "value": "taylorswift13"},
                     {"label": "Ronaldo", "value": "cristiano"}]
)
```

Listing 4-15: A Dropdown example not in twitter_app.py

Here we use the values as they appear in the DataFrame so that filtering is easier. But we can then choose a human-friendly representation for the label key to make it more recognizable to the user. When the user clicks on the dropdown, they will see the two options *Taylor* and *Ronaldo*, which are read by the app as taylorswift13 and cristiano, respectively.

The last Dropdown prop is value (not to be confused with the dictionary value key), and it consists of the default value the Dropdown will take when the user starts the app. Since we have a multivalue Dropdown, we use an initial value of three strings from the name column of the DataFrame: taylorswift13, cristiano, and jtimberlake.

These strings correspond to the values generated in the options prop in Listing 4-14. The strings are preloaded, so these three values are automatically chosen before the user even clicks the dropdown menu. Once the user chooses a different value in the dropdown menu, these values change accordingly.

For a complete video tutorial on the Dash Dropdown component and its usage, see the video "Dropdown Selector" at *https://learnplotlydash.com.*

Dash Callbacks

A *Dash callback* enables user interactivity within the dashboard app; it is the mechanism that connects the Dash components to each other so that performing one action causes something else to happen. When the app user selects a dropdown value, the figure is updated; when the user clicks a button, the color of the app's title changes or another graph is added to the page. The possible interactions between Dash components are infinite, and without callbacks, the app is static and the user cannot modify anything.

The Dash callback has two parts, the callback decorator that identifies the relevant components, defined in the layout section:

```
@app.callback()
```

and the callback function that defines how those Dash components should interact:

```
def function_name(y):
    return x
```

This simple app only has one callback, though more complicated apps will have many.

Callback Decorator

A callback decorator registers the callback function with your Dash app, telling it when to call the function and how to use the return value of the function to update the app. (We discussed decorators in Chapter 1.)

The callback decorator should be placed right above the callback function, and there must be no space between the decorator and the function. The decorator takes two main arguments: Output and Input, which refer to the component that should change (Output) in response to the user's action on a different component (Input). For example, the output might be the line chart, which should change depending on the user's input in the Dropdown component, as shown in Listing 4-16.

```
@app.callback(
    Output(component_id="line-chart", component_property="figure"),
    [Input(component_id="my-dropdown", component_property="value")],
)
```

Listing 4-16: A callback decorator from twitter_app.py

Both Output and Input take two arguments: component_id, which should correspond to the id of a particular Dash component, and component_property, which should correspond to a particular prop of that same component. In Listing 4-16, the component_id for Input refers to the my-dropdown Dropdown we defined earlier. The component_property refers specifically to the value prop of my-dropdown, which is the Twitter users' data to show, initially set to ["taylorswift13", "cristiano", "jtimberlake"], as in Listing 4-14.

In the Output we refer to the figure prop of dcc.Graph, which we also defined earlier in the layout, as shown in Listing 4-17.

```
dcc.Graph(id="line-chart", figure={})
```

Listing 4-17: The Graph component within the layout section in twitter_app.py

Here the figure prop is currently an empty dictionary, because the callback function will create a line chart based on the input and assign it to figure. Let's dive into the callback function to fully understand how this happens.

Callback Function

Our app's callback function, named update_graph(), holds a series of if-else statements that filter the DataFrame df and create a line chart depending on the input values chosen. Listing 4-18 shows the callback function in our app.

```
def update_graph(chosen_value):
    print(f"Values chosen by user: {chosen_value}")

    if len(chosen_value) == 0:
        return {}
    else:
```

```
df_filtered = df[df["name"].isin(chosen_value)]
fig = px.line(
    data_frame=df_filtered,
    x="date_time",
    y="number_of_likes",
    color="name",
    log_y=True,
    labels={
        "number_of_likes": "Likes",
        "date_time": "Date",
        "name": "Celebrity",
    },
)
return fig
```

Listing 4-18: The callback function in twitter_app.py

We'll go over the logic here line by line in a moment. First, though, let's discuss what this function achieves. When executed, update_graph() returns an object named fig, which in this case contains the Plotly Express line chart. The object fig is returned to the component and property we specified in Output in the callback decorator. As we know, the callback decorator refers to a Dash component in the layout. Here, then, fig is assigned to the figure prop of the Graph component in the layout section, so the callback is telling the app to display a line chart. Here's what the Graph component would look like after the callback function update_graph() executes:

```
dcc.Graph(id="line-chart", figure=fig)
```

The figure prop is now assigned the object fig instead of the empty dictionary we saw originally, in Listing 4-17.

We'll summarize this because this process is extremely important! Once the callback function is activated by user input, it returns an object that is tied to the component_property of the Output in the callback decorator. Given that the component property represents an actual prop of a component inside the app layout, the result is an app that is constantly being updated through user interaction.

For a complete video tutorial on the Dash callback decorator and its usage, see the video "The Dash Callback—Input, Output, State, and More" at *https://learnplotlydash.com*.

Activating the Callback

To activate the callback, the user must interact with the component specified in Input inside the callback decorator. In this app, the component property represents the value of the Dropdown, so every time the app user chooses a different dropdown value (a Twitter handle), the callback function is triggered.

If the callback decorator had three Inputs, the user would need to supply three arguments to trigger the callback function. In our case, the callback decorator has only one Input; therefore, the callback function will take only one argument: chosen_value.

How the Function Works

Let's examine Listing 4-19, which shows what is happening inside the app's callback function.

```
❶ def update_graph(chosen_value):
      print(f"Values chosen by user: {chosen_value}")

❷ if len(chosen_value) == 0:
      return {}
  else:
      df_filtered = df[df["name"].isin(chosen_value)]
      fig = px.line(
          data_frame=df_filtered,
          x="date_time",
          y="number_of_likes",
          color="name",
          log_y=True,
          labels={
              "number_of_likes": "Likes",
              "date_time": "Date",
              "name": "Celebrity",
          },
      )
      return fig
```

Listing 4-19: The callback function for twitter_app.py

The chosen_value argument ❶ refers to the value of the dcc.Dropdown, which is a list of Twitter usernames. Whenever a user chooses new options, the function is activated. The user can choose any number of available celebrities, and the number of items inside the chosen_value list will increase or decrease accordingly. It may be a list of 3 values, 10 values, or even no values. We therefore check the length of the chosen_value list ❷. If it is equal to zero and so is an empty list, the function returns an empty dictionary, and the fig object returned displays an empty graph.

If the length of the chosen_value list does not equal zero, in the else branch we use pandas to filter the DataFrame to only those rows that contain the selected Twitter usernames. The filtered DataFrame is saved to df_filtered and is then used as the data to create the line chart, which is saved as a fig object. The fig object is returned to display the line chart on the app page.

One important note on these functions: if the original DataFrame is altered in any way, you should always make a copy of the original DataFrame, as we did when we created df_filtered. The original DataFrame defined at the beginning of the app, in Listing 4-2, is considered a global variable. Global variables should never be altered, because doing so affects the variables seen by other users of the app. For example, if one user changed the global variable price_values in a financial dashboard app, all users would see these changed prices. This could cause significant damage and confusion.

Callback Diagram

Dash has a powerful callback diagram tool that displays the structure of the callback and delineates how elements are tied together. You should use this tool when defining callbacks, especially when they have multiple Inputs and Outputs, where it is harder to grasp the callback structure. To open the callback diagram, click the blue button in the bottom-right corner of the app page, shown in Figure 4-10.

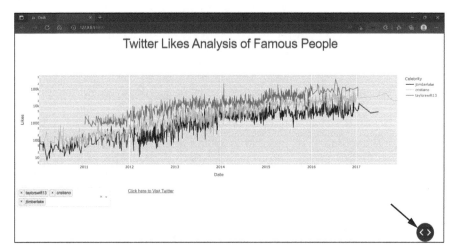

Figure 4-10: Click the button in the bottom-right corner to open the menu.

Then click the gray **Callbacks** button, shown in Figure 4-11.

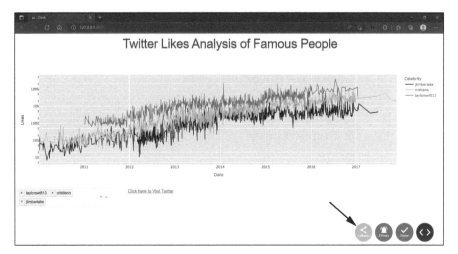

Figure 4-11: Click the Callbacks button to see the callback diagram.

The result should look like Figure 4-12.

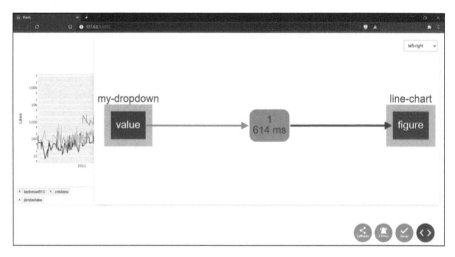

Figure 4-12: The callback diagram for twitter_app.py

The element on the left is the component property of the Input. The element in the middle describes the number of times the callback has been triggered in this session (once, in this case) as well as the time it took for the callback to fully execute (614 ms). The element on the right is the component property of the Output. The diagram helps paint a clear picture of how the Dropdown values (Input) influence the line chart's figure (Output).

Go ahead and trigger the callback by changing the Dropdown celebrity names on the main app page. See how the green element in the middle changes? Explore this diagram by clicking the left and right elements; you should see extra information within each element.

Make sure to turn debug mode off with debug = False before you deploy your app to the web in order to turn off the diagram. Otherwise, the end user will have access to the diagram as well.

Plotly Express Line Charts

Here we'll review how to create Plotly graphs. We'll focus on line charts, since that's what we use in this app, and we'll review other types of graphs in future chapters.

Plotly Express is a high-level interface for creating graphs quickly and intuitively. It contains dozens of figures to choose from, ranging from scientific, statistical, and financial graphs to 3D charts and maps. Every figure has numerous attributes that allow you to customize figures according to users' needs. Here's a complete list of the attributes available for the Plotly Express line chart, all currently set to None:

```
plotly.express.line(data_frame=None, x=None, y=None, line_group=None, color=None, line
_dash=None, hover_name=None, hover_data=None, custom_data=None, text=None, facet_row=None,
facet_col=None, facet_col_wrap=0, facet_row_spacing=None, facet_col_spacing=None, error_x=None,
error_x_minus=None, error_y=None, error_y_minus=None, animation_frame=None, animation_group
=None, category_orders={}, labels={}, orientation=None, color_discrete_sequence=None, color
_discrete_map={}, line_dash_sequence=None, line_dash_map={}, log_x=False, log_y=False, range_x
=None, range_y=None, line_shape=None, render_mode='auto', title=None, template=None,width
=None, height=None)
```

The beautiful thing about Plotly Express is that, in most cases, all you need to know to create a graph are the first three attributes: data_frame, x, and y, shown in bold in the example. These represent the DataFrame, the column of data to use for the x-axis, and the column to use for the y-axis, respectively. Here we plot a really simple line chart:

```
import plotly.express as px
px.line(data_frame=df, x="some_xaxis_data", y="some_yaxis_data")
fig.show()
```

This creates the most basic line chart, charting the relationship between two data columns, giving us something like Figure 4-13.

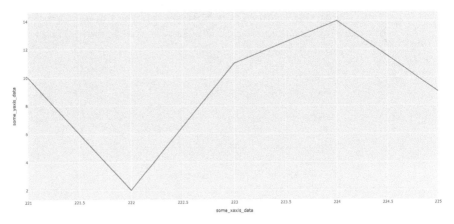

Figure 4-13: The simplest line chart

The more comfortable you become with Plotly Express, the more attributes you will find yourself adding to the figure. For example, to differentiate groups of data with color, we add the color attribute and assign it a column from the hypothetical DataFrame used:

```
px.line(data_frame=df, x="some_ xaxis _data", y="some_yaxis_data", color="some_data")
```

As a result, we would see something like Figure 4-14.

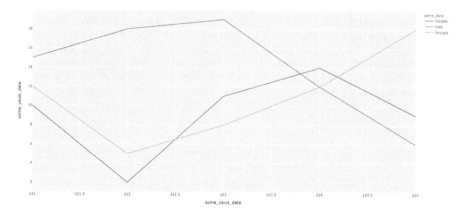

Figure 4-14: Adding a color *attribute to the simple chart*

To change the height of the figure, we add the `height` attribute and assign it a number of pixels:

```
px.line(data_frame=df, x="some_xaxis_data", y='some_yaxis_data', height=300)
```

Here we make the height of the entire graph 300 pixels.

In our Twitter Likes Analysis app, the line chart includes the `data_frame`, x, y, and color attributes, as well as the `labels` and `log_y` attributes. Listing 4-20 shows our Plotly chart code.

```
fig = px.line(
    data_frame=df_filtered,
    x="date_time",
    y="number_of_likes",
    color="name",
    log_y=True,
    labels={
        "number_of_likes": "Likes",
        "date_time": "Date",
        "name": "Celebrity",
    },
)
```

Listing 4-20: The Plotly line chart for twitter_app.py

The `log_y` attribute tells the app to use a logarithmic scale on the y-axis data. Logarithmic scaling is recommended when the chart has a few data points that are much larger or smaller than the bulk of the data, as it makes for a clearer visualization. We won't go into the details of logarithmic scales here, but try changing the attribute from `True` to `False` and then refresh the app to see the updated graph. Which one do you prefer?

The `labels` attribute changes the axis labels seen by the app users. The three columns used to plot the line chart are `date_time` (x-axis), `number_of_likes` (y-axis), and `name` (color). These are the names of the columns in the pandas

DataFrame, and we must maintain their format and spelling to match to the right column. With the `labels` attribute, we change what the user sees on the app page to make it more user friendly so that `number_of_likes` simply becomes `Likes`.

Each attribute is described in detail in the Plotly documentation at *https://plotly.com/python-api-reference*. It's worth spending time reading the descriptions because it will help you understand all the ways you can customize the line chart and other types of figures.

For a complete video tutorial on the Plotly Express line chart with `Dropdown`, see the video "Line Plot (Dropdown)" at *https://learnplotlydash.com*.

TOOL TIPS

There's one common attribute that we don't use in the app but is common enough that it's worth mentioning here: `hover_data`, which allows you to provide extra information in tool tips that appear when the user hovers over particular elements of the graph with the mouse cursor. You place the values assigned to `hover_data` inside a list or a dictionary.

When you use a list, the graph's hover tool tip will include the values in the list. For example, if we use the `number_of_shares` column as the `hover_data` list, the hover tool tip will include those pieces of data when the user hovers over the lines of our graph. To try this out, make the following change and rerun the app:

```
fig = px.line(data_frame=df_filtered, x="date_time", y="number_of_likes",
          color="name", hover_data=["number_of_shares"])
```

The following figure shows the difference in the hover information.

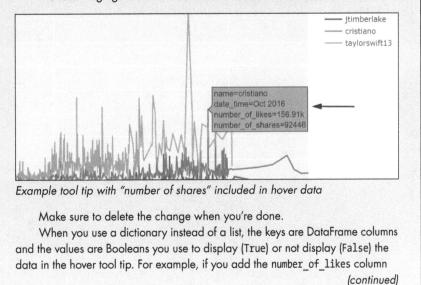

Example tool tip with "number of shares" included in hover data

Make sure to delete the change when you're done.

When you use a dictionary instead of a list, the keys are DataFrame columns and the values are Booleans you use to display (`True`) or not display (`False`) the data in the hover tool tip. For example, if you add the `number_of_likes` column

(continued)

---

as the dictionary key and `False` as the dictionary value, the data representing the number of likes per celebrity will no longer show in the hover tool tip:

```
hover_data={"number_of_likes": False}
```

We can also use the `hover_data` dictionary to format the hover data seen in the tool tip. For example, by default the `number_of_likes` is displayed with the letter "k" to represent 10,000 (200,000 is written as 200k). However, if we'd prefer to show the full number with a comma as the group separator (200,000), we would use:

```
hover_data={"number_of_likes": ':,'}
```

Summary

This chapter introduced you to the essential elements of a basic Dash app: Python libraries needed to program the app, the data used, Dash HTML and Core components, using the layout section to position the app components on the page, using callbacks to connect the components to each other and create interactivity, and the Plotly Express graphing library. In the next chapter we'll build on the skills learned here to develop more sophisticated Dash apps.

5

GLOBAL DATA ANALYSIS: ADVANCED LAYOUTS AND GRAPHS

In this chapter you'll expand your knowledge of Dash by building an app that compares and analyzes world data on three metrics: internet usage, proportion of females in parliament, and carbon dioxide (CO_2) emissions. We'll refer to these metrics as *indicators*. We'll look more closely at Dash callbacks, and you'll learn to plot a *choropleth map*, which represents quantitative data in the form of shades and colors within certain spatial areas on a map: countries, states, provinces, and so on. You'll also discover a new way to manage layout and styling using dash-bootstrap-components, a library that provides complex and responsive layouts.

To gather the data for this app, we'll access the World Bank application programming interface (API) using pandas. *APIs* provide an interface that allows you to connect to an external server and request data to feed into your app.

By the end of this chapter, you'll be a lot more comfortable plotting data on a map, managing more advanced layouts, understanding callbacks, and working with dash-core-components. But first things first: let's set up the app and the corresponding code.

Setting Up the Project

As usual, first you need to create your project folder and place the app code inside it. Create a new project folder called *world-bank-app*, and locate the *Chapter-5* folder included in the ZIP file you downloaded from *https://github.com/DashBookProject/Plotly-Dash* at the beginning of Chapter 4. The folder should contain two files: *worldbank.py* and *our_indicator.py*. Copy these files into your world-bank-app folder.

The project folder should look like this:

```
- world-bank-app
|--our_indicator.py
|--worldbank.py
```

We'll need four libraries: the usual pandas and Dash libraries, as well as dash-bootstrap-components and pandas datareader. Open your command prompt (Terminal for Mac users) or the Terminal tab in PyCharm or your Python IDE of choice. Then, line by line, enter the following to install the four libraries:

```
$ pip install pandas
$ pip install dash
$ pip install dash-bootstrap-components
$ pip install pandas-datareader
```

To check that the libraries have installed properly, enter:

```
$ pip list
```

This will list all Python packages you currently have installed. If any of the four libraries we need isn't listed, try reentering the corresponding install line.

Before we look at the code, let's check out the app. Open *worldbank.py* in your IDE and run the script. You should see a message with an HTTP link. Click that link or copy it into your web browser:

```
Dash is running on http://127.0.0.1:8050/
   * Serving Flask app "worldbank" (lazy loading)
   * Environment: production
     WARNING: This is a development server. Do not use it in a production
deployment.
```

```
  Use a production WSGI server instead.
* Debug mode: on
```

You should now see the World Bank Data Analysis dashboard app, as shown in Figure 5-1.

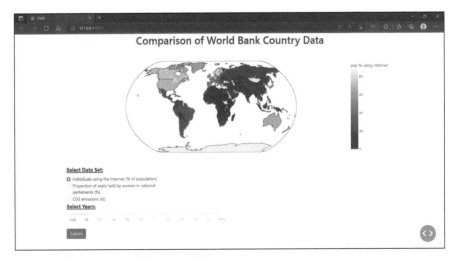

Figure 5-1: The World Bank Data Analysis app

Have a little fun! Use the slider to change the dates, and use the radio buttons to choose a different World Bank data indicator, such as the one for parliament seats or the one for CO_2 emissions. Move the map around and hover your mouse cursor over certain countries to compare their data. Which country has the highest percentage of females in parliament? Which country has seen the biggest growth in percentage of internet usage over time? Get familiar with the app, and the code should make more sense as we go through it.

Importing the Libraries

In this app we're introducing two new Python libraries: dash-bootstrap-components and pandas datareader.

dash-bootstrap-components is a package that makes it easier to manage the layout of the app. Bootstrap supplies components that allow you to do things like place app elements more precisely on a page, create more components like graphs and radio buttons, and style each element in very detailed ways. It's basically an add-on to the built-in Dash layout capabilities.

We'll use pandas to filter and prepare the data for plotting, as we did with the app in Chapter 4. This app, however, will also use pandas datareader, a pandas extension that retrieves data via APIs and creates DataFrames from that data. The pandas datareader extension has methods for extracting data from multiple common internet sources, such as NASDAQ, the Bank of Canada, the World Bank, and several more. Our app uses data from the World Bank only, so to access that data we need to import the wb World Bank module from the datareader extension, as shown in Listing 5-1.

```
import dash_bootstrap_components as dbc
from pandas_datareader import wb
```

Listing 5-1: The import section of the worldbank.py *app*

Data Management

The next section is the data management code, where we incorporate data into our app from the World Bank API. We'll also clean the data, taking out corrupt values, taking out corrupt values, extracting only the data we need, and merging it with another DataFrame to get the missing values.

Connecting to an API

Connecting to an API lets our app read data dynamically, allowing us to add and change the data we're reading on the fly, without having to alter and upload a static Excel file. By connecting to the API via pandas datareader, we can upload new data into the app immediately upon request.

It's important to note that some APIs enforce a limit on the number of requests an individual can make, in order to prevent an API from being overwhelmed. If that limit is surpassed, you may be blocked from making more requests for a certain amount of time. Taking timeouts between requests is one way to avoid overloading the API.

The wb module contains functions for getting different types of data pertaining to the World Bank. For example, the download() function will extract information from the World Bank's World Development Indicators when passed an indicator as an argument, while get_countries() will query information about specified countries. We will focus on these two for our app.

Let's start by downloading the necessary country data into our app, as shown in Listing 5-2.

```
countries = wb.get_countries()
countries["capitalCity"].replace({"": None}, inplace=True)
❶ countries.dropna(subset=["capitalCity"], inplace=True)
❷ countries = countries[["name", "iso3c"]]
countries = countries[countries["name"] != "Kosovo"]
countries = countries.rename(columns={"name": "country"})
```

Listing 5-2: Downloading country data from the World Bank API worldbank.py *app*

First we connect to the World Bank API and use get_countries() to extract the names of all the countries. However, the data isn't as clean as we'd like, and some of the rows actually contain names of regions rather than countries. For example, if you print the first 10 rows using the following:

```
countries = wb.get_countries()
print(countries.head(10)[['name']])
exit()
```

you will find that row 1 contains the "Africa Eastern and Southern" region. Our app is focused on just countries, so we use dropna() to exclude regions by dropping all rows that don't have a capital city ❶, which should leave us with country names only.

To plot points on a map Plotly uses country codes rather than country names, so next we need to provide the app with country codes. These codes are called *alpha-3* or *ISO3* codes, and each country has a different code. For example, Austria's is AUT, Azerbaijan's is AZE, Burundi's is BDI, and so on.

We don't need the other information get_countries() returns, so we limit the DataFrame to two necessary columns: the name column and the iso3c country code column ❷.

The authors' previous experiments with our app have shown that the ISO3 data for Kosovo is corrupt, so we filter the DataFrame to take out the Kosovo row. Lastly, we rename the name column to country to make the DataFrame easier to merge with another DataFrame later on (in Listing 5-4).

Identifying the Indicators

With the countries' DataFrame built, we need to extract the World Bank data tied to our three indicators: internet usage, female politicians, and emissions data. We first need to find the indicator's exact name and then find its respective ID so that we can query the API correctly. We get the indicator name directly from the World Bank website. Go to *https://data.worldbank .org/indicator*. To get the name for the internet usage indicator, click the **All Indicators** tab at the top of the page. Then, under the Infrastructure section, click **Individuals Using the Internet (% of Population)**. This is the exact name of the indicator we will be using in our app. If the World Bank website changes the names of the indicators, make sure you search for something similar and grab the exact name. We'll also keep the code in the book's resources up-to-date, if you get stuck.

Next we use the indicator name to get its ID using the *our_indicator.py* file you downloaded with the book's resources. In your project folder, open the *our_indicator.py* file in a new IDE window and run it:

```
df = wb.get_indicators()[['id','name']]
df = df[df.name == 'Individuals using the Internet (% of population)']
print(df)
```

This simply scrapes the entries from the name and id columns of the DataFrame pertaining to the World Bank site. The output should reveal the ID pertaining to that indicator:

	id	name
8045	IT.NET.USER.ZS	Individuals using the Internet (% of population)

You'll need to repeat this process to get the names for the remaining two indicators from the World Bank website by replacing 'Individuals using the Internet (% of population)' with the name of the other two indicators: 'Proportion of seats held by women in national parliaments (%)', found in the

Gender section, and 'CO2 emissions (kt)', found in the Climate Change section. Again, these names change every now and then, so if you don't get a result, make sure you search the World Bank indicators page and find the closest match. We then store the indicator names and IDs inside a dictionary located in the *worldbank.py* file, which we'll use later on, as shown in Listing 5-3.

```
indicators = {
    "IT.NET.USER.ZS": "Individuals using the Internet (% of population)",
    "SG.GEN.PARL.ZS": "Proportion of seats held by women in national parliaments (%)",
    "EN.ATM.CO2E.KT": "CO2 emissions (kt)",
}
```

Listing 5-3: Defining indicators inside worldbank.py

The main code you downloaded will have these IDs, but it's useful to practice retrieving them yourself since they do change from time to time.

Extracting the Data

Now we can build a function that downloads historical data for these three World Bank indicators, shown in Listing 5-4. We'll save the data in a new DataFrame called df.

```
def update_wb_data():
    # Retrieve specific world bank data from API
    df = wb.download(
        indicator=(list(indicators)), country=countries["iso3c"],
        start=2005, end=2016
    )
    df = df.reset_index()
    df.year = df.year.astype(int)

    # Add country ISO3 ID to main df
    df = pd.merge(df, countries, on="country")
    df = df.rename(columns=indicators)
    return df
```

Listing 5-4: The worldbank.py *section where historical data is downloaded*

We retrieve the data with the wb.download() method, which has a few parameters. The first is indicator, which takes a list of strings that represent the indicator IDs. Here we assign it the keys of the indicators dictionary from Listing 5-3. The next parameter is country, which takes a list of strings that represent the countries' ISO3 codes. We assign it the iso3c column of the countries DataFrame created in Listing 5-2. Lastly, the start and end parameters allow us to define the range of years for which we would like the data pulled. We stop at 2016 simply because that's the last year for which the World Bank has complete data for the CO_2 indicator.

We then reset the index so that country and year, which are part of the index, become new columns, and we have a dedicated index column with nothing but integers, which will help with filtering later. You can see the effect of resetting an index in Listing 5-5, where we showcase the DataFrame before and after resetting the index.

		IT.NET.USER.ZS	SG.GEN.PARL.ZS	EN.ATM.CO2E.KT
country	year			
Aruba	2016	93.542454	NaN	NaN
	2015	88.661227	NaN	NaN
	2014	83.780000	NaN	NaN
	2013	78.900000	NaN	NaN
	2012	74.000000	NaN	NaN
...	...	...	...	...
Zimbabwe	2009	4.000000	14.953271	7750.0
	2008	3.500000	15.238095	7600.0
	2007	3.000000	16.000000	9760.0
	2006	2.400000	16.666667	9830.0
	2005	2.400000	16.000000	10510.0

```
[2520 rows x 3 columns]

>>> df.reset_index()
```

	country	year	IT.NET.USER.ZS	SG.GEN.PARL.ZS	EN.ATM.CO2E.KT
0	Aruba	2016	93.542454	NaN	NaN
1	Aruba	2015	88.661227	NaN	NaN
2	Aruba	2014	83.780000	NaN	NaN
3	Aruba	2013	78.900000	NaN	NaN
4	Aruba	2012	74.000000	NaN	NaN
...	...	...	...	...	...
2515	Zimbabwe	2009	4.000000	14.953271	7750.0
2516	Zimbabwe	2008	3.500000	15.238095	7600.0
2517	Zimbabwe	2007	3.000000	16.000000	9760.0
2518	Zimbabwe	2006	2.400000	16.666667	9830.0
2519	Zimbabwe	2005	2.400000	16.000000	10510.0

```
[2520 rows x 5 columns]
```

Listing 5-5: The DataFrame before and after resetting the index

Before resetting the index, country and year were part of the index, but not part of the resultant row associated with an index element. After resetting the index, they are both individual columns of the DataFrame, which makes it a lot easier to access the individual rows that contain the country and year data.

Next we convert the values in the year column from strings to integers so that the data can be filtered correctly with pandas later on. The original df DataFrame does not contain the ISO3 country codes we need for querying the API, so we extract those codes from the countries DataFrame and merge the two DataFrames with pd.merge on the country column. Finally, we rename the columns so that they show the indicator names rather than the IDs, for human readability. For example, the column IT.NET.USER.ZS will now be named Individuals using the Internet (% of population).

The `update_wb_data()` function is now complete and will be called inside the first callback as soon as the app starts. You'll learn all about this process later in the chapter. In the meantime, let's learn how to use dash-bootstrap-components to create the layout and style the app.

Dash Bootstrap Styling

Dash Bootstrap is a powerful tool for styling Dash apps, helping us create the layout, style the app, and add Bootstrap components such as buttons and radio items. Buttons and radio items also exist in dash-core-components, but we'll use the dash-bootstrap-components versions for better compatibility with the rest of our Bootstrap styling. Bootstrap also contains modules that store items for various stylesheet themes as strings, which allows us to simply include links to those modules to style the elements.

To incorporate Bootstrap into the Dash app, we must first choose a theme and assign it to the `external_stylesheets` parameter right below our imports section, as shown in Listing 5-6.

```
import dash_bootstrap_components as dbc
from pandas_datareader import wb

app = Dash(__name__, external_stylesheets=[dbc.themes.BOOTSTRAP])
```

Listing 5-6: The worldbank.py *section where Dash is instantiated*

A Bootstrap theme is a stylesheet hosted online that determines the type of font, color, shape, and size of the elements on the page.

In this app, we use the default theme `BOOTSTRAP`, which is the first theme on the themes list. Bootstrap has several other themes at your disposal. To check out the themes, you can go to *https://hellodash.pythonanywhere.com* and click the **Change Theme** button on the left side of the page. You can switch up the theme for this app if you like; just make sure you use the exact name in capital letters when assigning it to the `external_stylesheets` parameter. You should only assign one theme at a time, so if you choose a new theme, make sure you replace `BOOTSTRAP`.

For a complete video tutorial on Dash Bootstrap, see the video "Complete Guide to Bootstrap Dashboard Apps" at *https://learnplotlydash.com*.

Layout

As you know, we generally refer to the layout of an app as a grid, which commonly consists of 12 columns and an infinite number of rows. To start building the layout, we need to create a container that will house all our rows and columns as well as the components that will go inside them. The `dbc.Container` syntax is pretty much like an `html.Div`, but it is more compatible with Bootstrap styling. First we'll declare the rows, then we'll declare the columns that go inside each row. Finally, we'll put the app components inside the columns. This final step defines the location of each component on the page.

To avoid overwhelming you with the 80 lines of code used to create the layout in our app, Listing 5-7 is a simplified version that removes the props within each html, dcc, and dbc component to just show the general structure.

```
app.layout = dbc.Container(
    [
      ❶ dbc.Row(
            dbc.Col(
                [
                    html.H1(),
                    dcc.Graph()
                ],
                width=12,
            )
        ),
      ❷ dbc.Row(
            dbc.Col(
                [
                    dbc.Label(),
                    dbc.RadioItems(),
                ],
                width=4,
            )
        ),
      ❸ dbc.Row(
            [
                dbc.Col(
                    [
                        dbc.Label(),
                        dcc.RangeSlider(),
                        dbc.Button()
                    ],
                    width=6,
                ),
            ]
        ),

    ]
)
```

Listing 5-7: App layout simplified

This app contains three rows. The first row ❶ has a column component that stretches 12 columns wide and contains the H1 heading and Graph visualization components. These correspond to the title and the choropleth map in the app, shown in Figure 5-1.

In the second row ❷ we place a column component that stretches only four columns wide, inside which we place the Label and RadioItems. These correspond to the "Select Data Set" subtitle and the three radio buttons beneath it in the app.

The last row ❸ contains the `Label`, `RangeSlider`, and `Button`, all of which are wrapped in a column component that is six columns wide.

MULTICOMPONENT ROWS

It's important to reiterate that an effective and popular approach to building dashboards is to set a maximum of 12 columns per page and allow components to span the width of multiple columns. In this app, each row has just one column component, but if we were to add several components in a row, we would have to make sure that, combined, they do not surpass the width of 12. Let's see an example:

```
dbc.Row([
    dbc.Col([dropdown, button, checkbox], width=6),
    dbc.Col([dropdown, slider, date-picker], width=5),
]),
```

In the preceding code, the total width is 11, which means that all the Dash components will be displayed on one row. Here's an example of what *not* to do:

```
dbc.Row([
    dbc.Col([dropdown, button, checkbox], width=8),
    dbc.Col([dropdown, slider, date-picker], width=6),
]),
```

With a total width of 14, the Dash components from the second `dbc.Col` will wrap into a row underneath the first `dbc.Col`, resulting in two rows instead of one. This can mess up your layout.

Components and Styling

Dash Bootstrap components are similar to Dash Core components, but with the advantage that they are easier to use and integrate with Bootstrap stylesheets. In our app, we use three Bootstrap components: `Label`, `RadioItems`, and `Button`. Let's look at the `Button` and `RadioItems` components.

We define the `Button` using five props: `id`, `children`, `n_clicks`, `color`, and `className`, as shown in Listing 5-8.

```
dbc.Button(
    id="my-button",
    children="Submit",
    n_clicks=0,
    color="primary",
    className="mt-4",
),
```

Listing 5-8: Defining a Bootstrap Button

The id prop is used to uniquely identify this component and will be assigned to the component_id inside the Dash callback to allow interaction with other components. Here we call it my-button. The children prop represents the text displayed on the button. The n_clicks prop counts the number of times the button has been clicked by the user, so we initialize it at 0. The color prop sets the color of the button background. Here it is assigned the Bootstrap contextual color primary, which represents the color blue (we could also use secondary to make it gray, success for green, warning for orange, or danger for red). Note that the color represented by primary depends on which theme you've chosen; if you were to choose the LUX theme for your Dash app, primary would represent the color black, and secondary would be white.

The className controls the styling of the component. Here we assign it the Bootstrap class mt-4, which controls how much margin there is between the top of the button and the component above it. The mt stands for *margin top*, and -4 creates four units of space in the margin above the component. All of this creates the button shown in Figure 5-2.

Submit

Figure 5-2: The Submit button for our app

Try changing the margin to mt-1 and see how the space shrinks between the button and the range slider above it.

You can also combine multiple classes within the className prop to add more styling by adding space between every additional class. For example, try adding fw-bold after mt-4 as one string to the className prop to make the Submit text bold, like so:

```
dbc.Button(
    id="my-button",
    children="Submit",
    n_clicks=0,
    color="primary",
    className="mt-4 fw-bold",
),
```

There are a few other Button props that we aren't using but are worth highlighting. The href prop can be assigned a URL, thereby taking the user to a new website once the button is clicked. The size prop controls the size of the button by assigning one of the following values: 'lg', 'md', or 'sm'. The disabled prop disables the button when we assign True to it; we might want to, for example, create a callback to instruct the app to disable the button if it's no longer needed.

Next we have RadioItems (also known as radio buttons), which are small circles or boxes next to a label that can be clicked. A radio button is similar to a checkbox except that, while the checkbox allows the user to choose multiple labels, the radio button only allows one label to be chosen at a time. The user will use it to choose which indicator they want to show the data for, as in Figure 5-3.

Select Data Set:

⦿ Individuals using the Internet (% of population)

○ Parliament seats % held by women

○ CO2 emissions (kt)

Figure 5-3: The indicator selection `RadioItems` *component*

We define the `RadioItems` with the four props shown in Listing 5-9.

```
dbc.RadioItems(
    id="radio-indicator",
❶ options=[{"label": i, "value": i} for i in indicators.values()],
❷ value=list(indicators.values()) [0],
    input_class_name="me-2",
),
```

Listing 5-9: The `RadioItems` *component in the layout section of* worldbank.py

We first give the `RadioItems` an id name. The `options` prop is responsible for displaying the labels. We pass it a list of dictionaries ❶, each of which represents a label; we use list comprehension to loop over all the indicators and create a label for each item. Alternatively, written out the long way in the following code, we could have assigned a list of three dictionaries to the `RadioItems` options prop like this (abridged) version. This would have achieved the exact same result:

```
options=[
    {"label": "Individuals using...", "value": "Individuals using..."},
    {"label": "Proportion of seats...", "value": "Proportion of seats..."},
    {"label": "CO2 emissions (kt)", "value": "CO2 emissions (kt)"}
]
```

Each dictionary has two keys: the `label` key determines the text to display to the user, while the `value` key is the actual value of the indicator. For example, we use the exact text "CO2 emissions (kt)" for the value in order to match the indicator's dictionary key value, as in Listing 5-3. This makes it a lot easier to filter the data later in the callback section. The `label` key can be anything you want to display, but here we use the same string for the `label` and the `value` since the string is already clear, informative, and not too long to display.

The next prop is value ❷, which registers the value selected by the user, depending on which radio button the user clicks; the object assigned to the `value` prop in Listing 5-9 represents the value chosen by default as the app loads for the first time. We use the `input_class_name` prop to style the radio button; in this case, we assign it the Bootstrap class `me-2` to set the circle two units of space to the left of the label. Try changing the number to see how this affects the appearance. Note that we can use Bootstrap classes to style Dash Core components, as well as Bootstrap components

There are innumerable Bootstrap classes, helpfully summarized and organized in the cheat sheet at *https://dashcheatsheet.pythonanywhere.com*. The `mt-4` class, for example, is located under the `Spacing` utility section, while `fw-bold` is located under the `Text` utility section. Play around with the other utilities and give the app your own personal style. We won't go over all the Bootstrap classes here, given the sheer number of them; instead, we recommend that you use the cheat sheet and experiment with incorporating different classes.

Always assign a Bootstrap theme to the `external_stylesheets` parameter, as we did in Listing 5-6, or the Bootstrap layout, styling, and elements will fail to function throughout the app.

Dash Core Components

We'll add a few new Dash Core components to the app, namely `RangeSlider`, `Store`, and `Interval`.

The `RangeSlider` is commonly used when we want to present a wide range of values to select from or when the user can select a range rather than discrete values. In this case, we'll use it to allow the user to select a single year or a range of years, as shown in Figure 5-4.

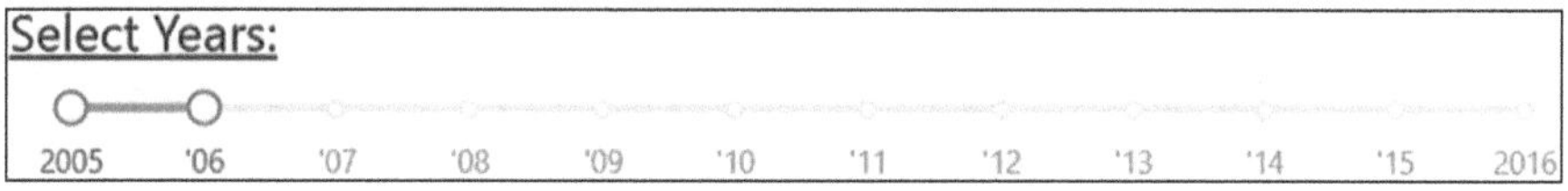

Figure 5-4: The years selection RangeSlider component

We'll define our `RangeSlider` with six props, as shown in Listing 5-10.

```
dcc.RangeSlider(
    id="years-range",
    min=2005,
    max=2016,
    step=1,
    value=[2005, 2006],
    marks={
        2005: "2005",
        2006: "'06",
        2007: "'07",
        2008: "'08",
        2009: "'09",
        2010: "'10",
```

```
                2011: "'11",
                2012: "'12",
                2013: "'13",
                2014: "'14",
                2015: "'15",
                2016: "2016",
            },
        ),
```

Listing 5-10: The RangeSlider *component in the layout section of* worldbank.py

The min and max props define the lowest and highest values on the RangeSlider, usually from left to right. The step prop determines the increment to make when the slider is moved. We set the value to 1 so that each movement of the slider will change the year by one. However, because we have marks for every year, assigning step to another value, say 3, would achieve the same result; the user's selection will automatically snap to the nearest mark. If we removed the marks for all the years between 2005 and 2016 and just kept those two, the slider would move to the nearest value in increments of three, assuming you assigned 3 to step.

The value prop determines the initial range that's selected by default when the app loads; it will also detect the range of years selected by the app user. The marks prop labels the marks. We assign it a dictionary: the key determines the position of the year on the slider, while the value indicates the text to display in that position on the app.

Another common RangeSlider prop, not used here, is allowCross, which allows the RangeSlider handles (the blue circles you see above 2005 and '06 in Figure 5-4) to cross each other when set to True. By default, allowCross=False, but if you changed that to True, you would be able to pull the 2005 handle to the right and over the '06 handle. For a full list of RangeSlider props, go to the Dash components documentation (*http://dash .plotly.com/dash-core-components*) and select dcc.RangeSlider. The props can be found at the bottom of the page. For a complete video tutorial on the Dash RangeSlider, see the video "Range Slider—Python Dash Plotly" at *https:// learnplotlydash.com*.

The Dash Store component is typically used to save dashboard data in memory on the user's web browser so that the data can be called and recalled quickly and efficiently. The store is invisible and does not appear on the user's page, though we must still declare it in the layout section, as shown in Listing 5-11.

```
dcc.Store(id="storage", storage_type="local", data={}),
```

Listing 5-11: The Store *component in the last section of the layout in* worldbank.py

This component allows for seamless and quick sharing of data between callbacks. There is a limit to the amount of data it can store, however: around 2MB of data in mobile environments and from 5MB to approximately 10MB in most desktop-only applications. We'll see how callbacks use the store in the next section.

The `id` prop will be used later in the callback to identify this component. The `data` prop represents the stored data; this data can be in the form of a dictionary, list, integer, string, or Boolean. We don't actually need to declare the `data` prop or assign an empty dictionary, as we did in Listing 5-11, but we've added it here for descriptive purposes. The `Store` component will always assume it's there, which is why we don't have to declare it.

The prop `storage_type` declares how we want to store the data. It has three options: `session`, `local`, and `memory`. The `session` option retains the data until the browser tab or the browser itself is closed and a new one is opened. The `local` option saves the data to the browser until all browsing history and cookies are deleted. The `memory` option resets the data when the browser is refreshed.

Our last component is the Dash `Interval`, used to automatically update the app without having to refresh the browser page manually. This is typically used with apps that use data in real time, such as financial apps, which need to update themselves with new data every couple of seconds. In our app, the `Interval` activates the first callback, which itself creates the DataFrame from the data pulled from the World Bank pandas API. Then, every 60 seconds, the `Interval` reactivates the callback to pull the data again and create a new DataFrame.

The `Interval` has a few important props, shown in Listing 5-12.

```
dcc.Interval(id="timer", interval=1000 * 60, n_intervals=0),
```

Listing 5-12: The Interval component in the last section of the layout in worldbank.py

The `interval` prop tells the app how much time should transpire between every activation of the `Interval`. We assign this interval in milliseconds, so here we use `1000 * 60`, which is equal to 60 seconds. Every 60 seconds you should see the word "Updating" appear in the browser's window tab. The `n_intervals` prop counts the number of times the `Interval` has been activated: after 60 seconds `n_intervals=1`, after 120 seconds `n_intervals=2`, and so on until the end of time. One other common prop not presented here is `max_intervals`, which defines the maximum number of times `Interval` will be activated. If, for example, `max_intervals=2` and `interval=1000*60`, the app will stop updating itself after 120 seconds.

In reality, we don't really need to update the data every 60 seconds, because the World Bank probably only updates its data every couple of weeks. We simply chose 60-second intervals so that you can see the `Interval` component in action.

For a complete video tutorial on the Dash `Interval`, see the video "The Dash Interval Overview" at *https://learnplotlydash.com.*

Dash Callbacks

Our app uses two callbacks. The first callback is responsible for retrieving data from the World Bank through the pandas datareader API, while the second callback is responsible for creating and displaying the choropleth map on the app.

Data Retrieval Callback

The data retrieval callback will call on the appropriate components to retrieve the chosen data every 60 seconds and return a DataFrame of that data, which is stored on the user's web browser. As always, the callback has two sections: the callback decorator and the callback function, as shown in Listing 5-13.

```
❶ @app.callback(Output("storage", "data"), Input("timer", "n_intervals"))
❷ def store_data(n_time):
       dataframe = update_wb_data()
       return dataframe.to_dict("records")
```

Listing 5-13: The first callback in worldbank.py

Within the callback decorator ❶ the Input and Output parameters take a component_id and a component_property, whose assigned values refer to components in the layout section of the app. The component_id of the Input parameter in this case is "timer", and the component_property refers to "n_intervals". These are positional arguments, so we don't need to include the parameters in the decorator function code. In fact, the same line of code written the long way would look like this:

```
@app.callback(
    Output(component_id="storage", component_property="data"),
    Input(component_id="timer", component_property="n_intervals")
)
```

As shown in Listing 5-13, "timer" refers to the id of the Dash Interval component and "n_intervals" refers to the prop that represents the number of times the Interval has been fired. Following the same logic, "storage" refers to the id of the Dash Store component and "data" refers to the prop that represents the data being stored on the user's browser.

Inside the callback function ❷ we pass in the single Input argument n_time. The n_time argument refers to the value assigned to Input's component_property, which is n_intervals. Because n_time refers to n_intervals, every time the Interval is triggered (every 60 seconds) the callback function will be triggered as well. The first trigger occurs as soon as the app is rendered on the page for the first time or as soon as the page is refreshed.

You can call this argument anything you'd like; it doesn't have to be called n_time. However, it's important to note that only one argument is passed into the callback function because the callback decorator only has one Input.

Once the function is triggered, it activates the update_wb_data function at the beginning of the app (Listing 5-4), and it saves the results to the dataframe object. This DataFrame now contains data from the World Bank. The DataFrame is then returned. Every object returned in the callback function corresponds to the `component_property` of the `Output` argument. In this case, the returned DataFrame corresponds to the `data` prop of the `Store` component, as seen in Listing 5-13. As a result, the retrieved World Bank data is stored on the user's web browser for future use.

Our callback decorator has only one output, so one object is returned in the callback function. In apps where the callback decorator has multiple outputs, you will have to return the same number of objects in the callback function. For example, here the callback function returns two messages because the decorator function has two outputs:

```
@app.callback(
    Output("example-content1", "children"),
    Output("example-content2", "children"),
    Input("timer", "n_intervals")
)
def update_data(n_time):
    message1 = "text to display in the children prop of the 1st Output."
    message2 = "text to display in the children prop of the 2nd Output."

    return message1, message2
```

For a complete video tutorial on the Dash callback function, see the video "The Dash Callback—Input, Output, State, and more" at *https://learnplotlydash.com.*

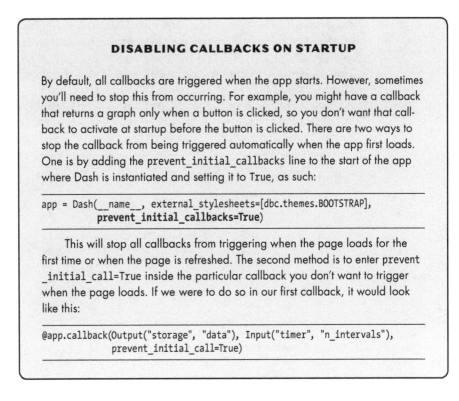

DISABLING CALLBACKS ON STARTUP

By default, all callbacks are triggered when the app starts. However, sometimes you'll need to stop this from occurring. For example, you might have a callback that returns a graph only when a button is clicked, so you don't want that callback to activate at startup before the button is clicked. There are two ways to stop the callback from being triggered automatically when the app first loads. One is by adding the `prevent_initial_callbacks` line to the start of the app where Dash is instantiated and setting it to True, as such:

```
app = Dash(__name__, external_stylesheets=[dbc.themes.BOOTSTRAP],
        prevent_initial_callbacks=True)
```

This will stop all callbacks from triggering when the page loads for the first time or when the page is refreshed. The second method is to enter `prevent_initial_call=True` inside the particular callback you don't want to trigger when the page loads. If we were to do so in our first callback, it would look like this:

```
@app.callback(Output("storage", "data"), Input("timer", "n_intervals"),
        prevent_initial_call=True)
```

Figure Creation Callback

The figure creation callback will retrieve the stored DataFrame from the user's browser, filter the DataFrame based on the years and dataset selected by the user, and return a graph that represents that data visually. The decorator function has two Input arguments, two State arguments, and one Output, as seen in Listing 5-14.

```
@app.callback(
    Output("my-choropleth", "figure"),
    Input("my-button", "n_clicks"),
    Input("storage", "data"),
    State("years-range", "value"),
    State("radio-indicator", "value"),
)
```

Listing 5-14: The callback decorator of the second callback in worldbank.py

The first Input refers to the number of times the button is clicked, and the second refers to the data stored on the user's browser by the first callback. Next we define a couple of State arguments. A State argument doesn't trigger the callback when its components are altered, but rather makes note of the user's selection. Here, the first State argument checks which range of years the user has chosen on the RangeSlider, and the second one refers to the indicator chosen from the RadioItems.

When the user changes the year(s) selected on the RangeSlider or chooses a different RadioItems World Bank indicator, the values are saved, but the choropleth map does not update until the button is clicked. This is because the button's n_clicks is a component property of an Input argument (Listing 5-14). Remember, Input arguments always trigger callbacks. State arguments do not.

Now let's look at the callback function. The callback decorator has four arguments that are not Outputs, so the callback function must also be assigned four arguments, as shown in Listing 5-15.

```
def update_graph(n_clicks, stored_dataframe, years_chosen, indct_chosen):
❶   dff = pd.DataFrame.from_records(stored_dataframe)
    print(years_chosen)

❷   if years_chosen[0] != years_chosen[1]:
❸       dff = dff[dff.year.between(years_chosen[0], years_chosen[1])]
❹       dff = dff.groupby(["iso3c", "country"])[indct_chosen].mean()
        dff = dff.reset_index()

        fig = px.choropleth(
            data_frame=dff,
            locations="iso3c",
            color=indct_chosen,
            scope="world",
            hover_data={"iso3c": False, "country": True},
            labels={
```

```
        indicators["SG.GEN.PARL.ZS"]: "% parliament women",
        indicators["IT.NET.USER.ZS"]: "pop % using internet",
      },
    )
    fig.update_layout(
        geo={"projection": {"type": "natural earth"}},
        margin=dict(l=50, r=50, t=50, b=50),
    )
    return fig

❺ if years_chosen[0] == years_chosen[1]:
  ❻     dff = dff[dff["year"].isin(years_chosen)]
  ❼     fig = px.choropleth(
          data_frame=dff,
          locations="iso3c",
          color=indct_chosen,
          scope="world",
          hover_data={"iso3c": False, "country": True},
          labels={
              indicators["SG.GEN.PARL.ZS"]: "% parliament women",
              indicators["IT.NET.USER.ZS"]: "pop % using internet",
          },
      )
      fig.update_layout(
          geo={"projection": {"type": "natural earth"}},
          margin=dict(l=50, r=50, t=50, b=50),
      )
      return fig
```

Listing 5-15: Defining the callback function of the second callback in worldbank.py

The four arguments correspond to the component properties of State and Input in Listing 5-14 in the following manner:

n_clicks to n_clicks

stored_dataframe to data

years_chosen to value

indct_chosen to value

The first line of code within the callback function ❶ converts the stored data, which is currently a list of dictionaries, to a pandas DataFrame to make it easier to create the Plotly Express graphs.

We next need to filter the data to prepare it for plotting the choropleth map. To see how best to filter the RangeSlider data, go to the app and try to move the slider handles to select multiple years or only one year and hit **Submit**. See what's then printed out in the Python IDE. You should see something like this:

```
[2005, 2006]
[2005, 2009]
[2009, 2009]
```

We can see that the app must distinguish whether the two values in the years_chosen list are different from each other ❷ or the same ❺ so that it knows whether to use data from a range or a single year. Now that we know what the data looks like, it's easier to filter.

If the two values are different, it means the user has selected a range. First we create a DataFrame that is limited to only those rows pertaining to the range of years selected by the user ❸. If the user moved the slider handles to choose [2005, 2009], the new DataFrame will include all the years between 2005 and 2009. Next, for each country we extract the mean value for the indicator chosen. Because each country appears multiple times on multiple rows—once for each year—we also group the DataFrame by the country and iso3c columns ❹. This ensures that each country will be represented only once in the new DataFrame.

If you're not sure what certain lines of code do, add print statements between the lines to clarify what the data looks like before and after each manipulation.

If the two values in the years_chosen list are the same ❺, it means the user selected only one year (for example, [2009, 2009]). Consequently, there is no need to use groupby, because every country will appear only once. Lastly, we filter the DataFrame so that it contains only rows with the selected year ❻.

With the data fully filtered, it is now ready to be used to plot the choropleth map. We will use the last section of this chapter, "Plotly Express Choropleth Maps," to go over the creation of the choropleth ❼.

Callback Diagram

To depict more clearly what's happening in the callbacks, we'll look at the callback diagram, as we did in Chapter 4, to get information on the order in which the callbacks are triggered, the amount of time it takes to fully render each callback, and the component within the callback that's being activated.

First, as shown in Listing 5-16, reduce the interval in the layout section to 10 seconds so that the callback is triggered more frequently and you can see what's happening in the callback diagram every 10 seconds. Also check that debug=True at the end of the code; otherwise, the diagram won't appear.

```
dcc.Interval(id="timer", interval=1000 * 10, n_intervals=0),

if __name__ == "__main__":
    app.run_server(debug=True)
```

Listing 5-16: The Interval component and the last line of code in worldbank.py

Now run the app, and in the browser click the **Callbacks** button in the lower-right corner. Figure 5-5 shows the diagram that should appear.

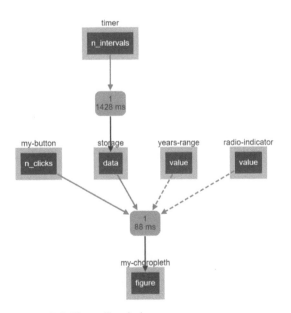

Figure 5-5: The callback diagram

Each callback argument (`Input`, `Output`, or `State`) is represented by a box, and another box tells you the number of times a callback was triggered and how quickly. As you can see, the first input refers to the `Interval` component. The box in the second row tells us that the callback has been triggered once (when the page loaded), and that it took a little over one second (1,428 milliseconds) to complete the callback and store the data on the browser. Observe how the arrow from that box points to the storage component in the third row. You should see the top digit in the box in the second row increase by one every 10 seconds.

The four boxes in the third row represent the two `Input` and two `State` arguments in the second callback. The box beneath informs us that the second callback has been triggered once and that it took less than one-tenth of a second to return a figure of the choropleth map as an `Output`.

Approximately one second after the first callback is complete, you should see the outline of the storage component highlighted in purple on your screen. This is because the storage component activates the second callback.

Let's see how the diagram changes as the user interacts with the app. Click the button, choose a different `RadioItem`, and move the years of the `RangeSlider`. Whenever you interact with a component, its respective blue box in the diagram should highlight. Notice how the `RadioItem` and the `RangeSlider` do not trigger the second callback; only the `Button` and `Store` components trigger the second callback because they are `Input` arguments, as opposed to `State` arguments.

Don't forget to change the interval in the layout section back to 60 seconds to avoid overloading the API with requests.

Callback Ordering

Before we move on, it's important to discuss the order in which we write callbacks. If callbacks do not depend on each other, the order does not matter because when the page first loads, the callbacks can be called in any order. However, for callbacks that do depend on each other, as they do in this app, the writing order is important. The callback that needs to be triggered first should be written above any callbacks that depend on it; accordingly, we placed the callback that stores the data above the callback that uses the stored data to plot the figure.

For a complete video tutorial on Dash chained callbacks, see the video "Chained Callback in Dash" at *https://learnplotlydash.com.*

Plotly Express Choropleth Maps

The choropleth map represents quantitative data in shades and colors over a map of certain spatial areas. The choropleth map is a great data visualization tool for displaying variations in data across regions. The earliest known choropleth map was created by Charles Dupin in 1826 to depict the availability of basic education in departments of France, as seen in Figure 5-6. Choropleths were first referred to as *cartes teintées,* or "color maps."

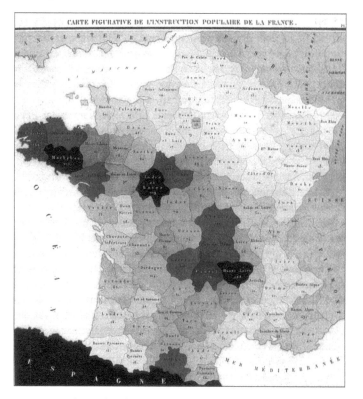

Figure 5-6: The earliest known choropleth map (Source: https://en.wikipedia.org/wiki/Choropleth_map)

We visualize our data as a choropleth using the Plotly Express method px.choropleth. Here is a complete list of the attributes pertaining to the choropleth map in Plotly Express:

```
plotly.express.choropleth(data_frame=None, lat=None, lon=None, locations=None, locationmode=None,
geojson=None, featureidkey=None, color=None, facet_row=None, facet_col=None, facet_col_wrap=0,
facet_row_spacing=None, facet_col_spacing=None, hover_name=None, hover_data=None, custom
_data=None, animation_frame=None, animation_group=None, category_orders=None, labels=None, color
_discrete_sequence=None, color_discrete_map=None, color_continuous_scale=None, range_color=None,
color_continuous_midpoint=None, projection=None, scope=None, center=None, fitbounds=None,
basemap_visible=None, title=None, template=None, width=None, height=None)
```

To build our choropleth, we only need six of these attributes, as shown in Listing 5-17.

```
fig = px.choropleth(
    data_frame=dff,
    locations="iso3c",
    color=indct_chosen,
    scope="world",
    hover_data={"iso3c": False, "country": True},
    labels={indicators["SG.GEN.PARL.ZS"]: "% parliament women",
            indicators["IT.NET.USER.ZS"]: "pop % using internet"},
)
```

Listing 5-17: The choropleth figure inside the second callback function of worldbank.py

To the data_frame attribute we assign the dataset we filtered earlier, according to the years_chosen argument. To locations we assign the iso3c column, which contains three-letter country codes as defined at the Natural Earth website (*https://www.naturalearthdata.com*). The color attribute controls how the map uses color distinctions. We pass it indct_chosen, which corresponds to the indicator that the user chooses from the RadioItem.

The scope attribute describes the area of the map that the figure will feature, and has specific keywords we can assign to it: world, usa, africa, asia, europe, north america, or south america. For example, if the data plotted was only for Africa, the scope chosen should be africa instead of world. Here we choose the whole world. The hover_data attribute controls what information appears in the tool tips when the user hovers their mouse over the map. Here we assign "country": True to show the country names but hide the country codes. The labels attribute instructs the app to change the names of certain columns. Because in this case the names are used in the hover tool tip and in the title of the color bar to the right of the graph, space is limited. We therefore change the names of the labels so that they are shorter and can fit in their respective displayed location in the app.

To manipulate certain aspects of the choropleth layout, we must turn to Plotly Graph Objects: the low-level interface for creating graphs from the bottom up. Given that Plotly Express is built on top of Plotly Graph Objects, anytime a figure needs more elaborate customization features that don't exist in Plotly Express, you can use figure attributes from Graph Objects. In

Listing 5-18, we use it to change the displayed shape of the map and reduce the empty margin space around it, thereby enlarging the map itself.

```
fig.update_layout(
    geo={"projection": {"type": "natural earth"}},
    margin=dict(l=50, r=50, t=50, b=50),
)
```

Listing 5-18: Updating the layout of the choropleth figure inside the second callback function of worldbank.py

The geo attribute can take many dictionary keys that are responsible for changing the layout of the map, including projection, oceancolor, and resolution, among others. The projection key has its own dictionary key called type, which determines the shape of the frame for the map. Assigning natural earth to the type key displays the map in an oblong frame instead of a boxed frame. Try changing natural earth to satellite or bonne and see how the shape of the map is altered. The second attribute, margin, enlarges the map size displayed by reducing the margins from the default of 80 pixels to 50 pixels. A complete list of the Plotly Graph Objects attributes for choropleths is available at *https://plotly.com/python/reference/choropleth.*

Summary

In this chapter you learned several new concepts: you learned to use pandas datareader to extract data from the web; you were introduced to Dash Bootstrap components to manage the layout and styling of an app and to some new and important Dash Core components, such as Store and Interval; you learned how to create an app with multiple callbacks; and you dove headfirst into the trendy choropleth map. With these skills, you can create ever more effective and complex dashboards that update in real time.

6

INVESTMENT PORTFOLIO: BUILDING LARGER APPS

In this chapter we'll show you how to create an investment portfolio app that explores how asset allocation affects a portfolio's return. We'll start with an introduction to asset allocation and why it's an important concept in investing. We'll then create a dashboard to explore a dataset detailing annual returns for cash, stocks, and bonds since 1929. The app will show you how interactive dashboards created with Dash really help bring data to life.

This app contains more lines of code than the app in Chapter 5. We'll introduce ways to organize larger apps and offer some tips and tricks for maintaining and debugging large apps. We also cover some advanced callback techniques.

By the end of this chapter, you'll know how to:

- Structure a larger project to make it easier to maintain and debug
- Include FontAwesome icons in your app
- Use new Dash Core components: `DataTable`, `Slider`, and `Markdown`
- Use new Dash Bootstrap components: `Card`, `InputGroup`, `Table`, `Tabs`, and `Tooltip`
- Use Plotly Graph Objects to make color-coded figures

We'll also cover some advanced callback techniques, such as using callbacks with multiple inputs and outputs, getting data from components without triggering a callback, and synchronizing components using callbacks. Before we get to the code, though, you'll need a little background on asset allocation.

Asset Allocation

One of the primary goals in investing is to obtain the highest returns with the lowest risk of loss. *Asset allocation* is the strategy of dividing an investment portfolio among different categories of assets such as stocks, bonds, and cash. The objective is to reduce risk through diversification. Historically, the returns of these asset classes do not move in unison. For example, when stocks are down, bonds are often up. Having both classes in your portfolio can reduce risk since they offset each other.

The amount to allocate to each asset class depends on your goals, time horizon, and risk tolerance. For example, stocks are more volatile than bonds or cash but typically have higher returns in the long run. If you are investing for a retirement that's decades in the future, you may be comfortable allocating more of your portfolio to stocks since you have time to wait out the inevitable ups and downs of the market. That said, it's hard to know ahead of time how you'll feel when you see the balance in your account decline, and it's not uncommon for people to panic when they see their stocks drop and sell them at the bottom of the market, locking in those losses. Having other assets that don't decline at the same time as stocks can help you stick with your long-term strategy.

There are risks in being too conservative as well. If you have too much allocated to cash, you are at risk of not having enough funds at retirement. However, for short-term goals such as being able to cover unexpected living expenses, it's appropriate to hold cash.

If you are new to investing and this isn't making much sense, playing with the app can help clarify these concepts. That's one of the great things about data visualization. With a glance at the color-coded graph, you can see how stocks, bonds, and cash have performed over time. This app will analyze and graphically depict how asset allocation affects your chosen portfolio, allowing you to tweak your allocation ratios to see how portfolios with various allocations perform over time.

Download and Run the App

First let's take a look at the finished app. You'll find the full code at *https://github.com/DashBookProject/Plotly-Dash*. Download and run it locally using the instructions in Chapter 2, or see it live at *https://wealthdashboard.app*. Figure 6-1 shows a screenshot of the app.

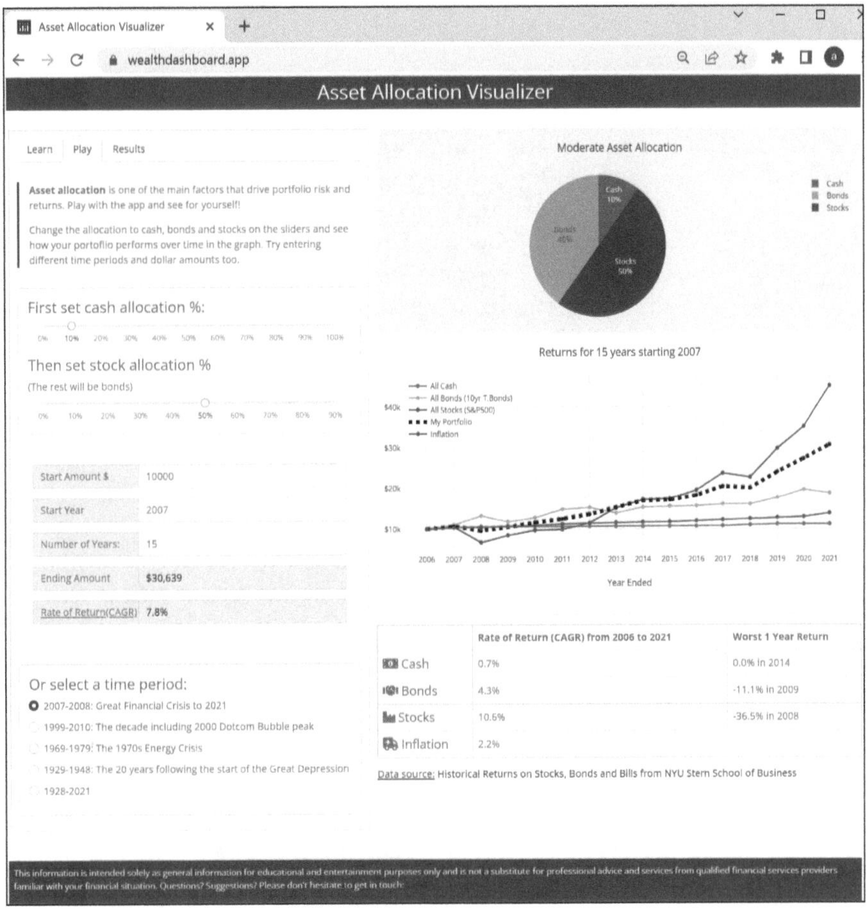

Figure 6-1: Screenshot of the Asset Allocation Visualizer app

You can see there are a lot more elements in this app than in our previous Dash apps. Try using the app to see how it functions. Enter different numbers in the input fields. Move the sliders to select different asset allocations. See what your investment returns would be if you put all your money in cash, or stocks, or bonds, or various combinations of the three. Use the radio buttons to select different time periods to see how your portfolio would have performed if you had started investing at the height of the dotcom bubble or the depths of the Great Depression.

Notice how the components in the app interact and how the pie chart, line chart, tables, and results fields update. You'll learn how to do this in the "Dash Callbacks" section later in this chapter.

Also, take note of the layout design. This app has sliders, input fields, and checklist options on the left side and output in the form of a pie chart, line chart, and summary table on the right. You will learn how to do this later in this chapter, in the "Layout and Styling" section.

App Structure

One remarkable thing about Dash is how easy it is to make visual, interactive apps with just a few lines of code. The first two apps in this book are good examples, and you can see more in the Dash tutorial and in the Dash Enterprise App Gallery. However, when you start making your own apps, you'll find it's easy for the code to grow and become hundreds or even thousands of lines long as you add more features and components and build multipage apps. This chapter's app has about 700 lines of code, and it is still relatively simple.

When you start working with larger apps, you'll quickly understand why structuring your app is important. In small apps, it can be convenient to do things like define components directly in the layout or even in a callback, but as you add more features, this method can make your layout huge and difficult to manage, change, and debug.

In larger apps, we might separate sections into their own files. In this app, since it's still relatively small, we keep all the code in one file but organize it so that related elements are grouped together. For example, we have different sections for figures, tables, tabs, and Markdown components. Each component is either defined in a function or assigned a variable name. Because the components are structured in this way, they become building blocks that we can then place in the layout as and when we need them by using a function call or calling the variable name. This organization also makes it easy to reuse these components in other apps. We split out the helper functions that do the data wrangling, such as calculating the investment returns, into their own section too. We're able to keep the layout section concise at only 30 lines of code because of the way we structured the components. The last section has the app callbacks.

There are many ways to structure an app. You could, for instance, put some sections in different modules and import them into the main app. For multipage apps, it's standard practice to have each page in a different module. You will see examples of this in Chapter 7. The important thing is to have a consistent method of organizing and structuring your app that works for you and makes sense for the project. For this app, given the size and that it's a single-page app, we prefer to keep everything together.

Setting Up the Project

As usual, we'll open with importing the libraries and managing the data.

Importing the Libraries

We start by importing the modules we use in the app (Listing 6-1). New to this app are the data_table, State, callback_context, and plotly.graph_objects modules.

```
from dash import Dash, dcc, html, dash_table, Input, Output, State, callback_context
import dash_bootstrap_components as dbc
import plotly.graph_objects as go
import pandas as pd
```

Listing 6-1: The import section of app.py

We use data_table to display results and source data. We use State and callback_context in our callbacks, and we use Plotly Graph Objects rather than Plotly Express to create the figures. We will discuss each of these in more detail later.

Adding the Stylesheets

Next we will add the Bootstrap CSS and the FontAwesome icons as external stylesheets. In Chapter 5 we added the BOOTSTRAP theme to the app, and in this app we use the SPACELAB theme, like so:

```
app = Dash(__name__, external_stylesheets=[dbc.themes.SPACELAB, dbc.icons.FONT_AWESOME])
```

The SPACELAB theme provides us with the fonts, color palette, shapes, and sizes of the page elements you see in Figure 6-1.

The FontAwesome library has an extensive collection of icons to help make an app more eye-catching. Figure 6-2 shows the FontAwesome icons we use in the app.

	Rate of Return (CAGR) from 2006 to 2021	Worst 1 Year Return
Cash	0.7%	0.0% in 2014
Bonds	4.3%	-11.1% in 2009
Stocks	10.6%	-36.5% in 2008
Inflation	2.2%	

Figure 6-2: The FontAwesome icons we use in the app

The Dash Bootstrap Components library has a module with the URLs for the FontAwesome and Bootstrap icons plus the URLs for various Bootstrap themes. This makes it easier to add them to your app. For example, you can specify the theme as dbc.themes.SPACELAB rather than *https://cdn.jsdelivr.net/npm/bootswatch@5.1.3/dist/spacelab/bootstrap.min.css*.

Data Management

The data source for this app comes from Professor Aswath Damodaran, who teaches corporate finance and valuation at the Stern School of Business at New York University. It includes the returns for three asset classes—cash, bonds, and stocks—represented by the three-month US Treasury Bill, the 10-year US Treasury Bond, and the S&P 500. You can learn more about this data at *http://people.stern.nyu.edu/adamodar/New_Home _Page/data.html*.

We've downloaded the data and saved it as an Excel spreadsheet named *historic.csv* in the *assets* folder. Here we include the data in our app:

```
df = pd.read_csv("assets/historic.csv")
```

Next we take some steps to make the app easier to maintain over time. First we make the start and end years of the data series global variables, since we use these dates in numerous places in the app. Now when we update the app annually with new data, we don't have to make any changes to the code for the new dates:

```
MAX_YR = df.Year.max()
MIN_YR = df.Year.min()
START_YR = 2007
```

The START_YR is the default starting year for the investment period when the app first runs. Rather than hardcoding "2007" into various places in the app, we use this global variable. If you decide you want a different start year, you only need to change it in this one line of code.

We also make the colors global variables. We use custom colors for the stocks, bonds, and cash in the graphs, picked to match our Bootstrap theme. If you want to change to a different Bootstrap theme, you can update the graph colors by changing the color numbers here in the COLORS dictionary, and the colors will be updated throughout the app:

```
COLORS = {
    "cash": "#3cb521",
    "bonds": "#fd7e14",
    "stocks": "#446e9b",
    "inflation": "#cd0200",
    "background": "whitesmoke",
}
```

Using this dictionary also makes the code more readable and self-documenting, since you can specify a color like this:

```
COLORS["stocks"]
```

rather than like this:

```
"#446e9b"
```

Layout and Styling

In this section we'll separate out all components and figures to modularize them so that we can add them to the layout wherever we like, as mentioned at the start of the chapter. The main layout comprises only about 30 lines of the app's 700 lines of code. To keep it this short we define the components and figures in another section of the app and give them variable names that we can call in the layout section. Structuring the layout in this way clarifies the app structure and simplifies design changes.

Listing 6-2 shows the `app.layout` code for the main layout.

```
app.layout = dbc.Container(
    [
    ❶ dbc.Row(
            dbc.Col(
                html.H2(
                    "Asset Allocation Visualizer",
                    className="text-center bg-primary text-white p-2",
                ),
            )
        ),
    ❷ dbc.Row(
            [
                dbc.Col(tabs, width=12, lg=5, className="mt-4 border"),
                dbc.Col(
                    [
                        dcc.Graph(id="allocation_pie_chart", className="mb-2"),
                        dcc.Graph(id="returns_chart", className="pb-4"),
                        html.Hr(),
                        html.Div(id="summary_table"),
                        html.H6(datasource_text, className="my-2"),
                    ],
                    width=12,
                    lg=7,
                    className="pt-4",
                ),
            ],
            className="ms-1",
        ),
        dbc.Row(dbc.Col(footer)),
    ],
    ❸ fluid=True,
)
```

Listing 6-2: Layout code

The entire app content is wrapped in a `dbc.Container`, the most basic layout element in Bootstrap that's required when using the rows and columns grid system.

The first row ❶ of the layout defines the blue header bar, shown in Figure 6-3, which is defined as a Bootstrap row with one column that spans the entire width of the screen.

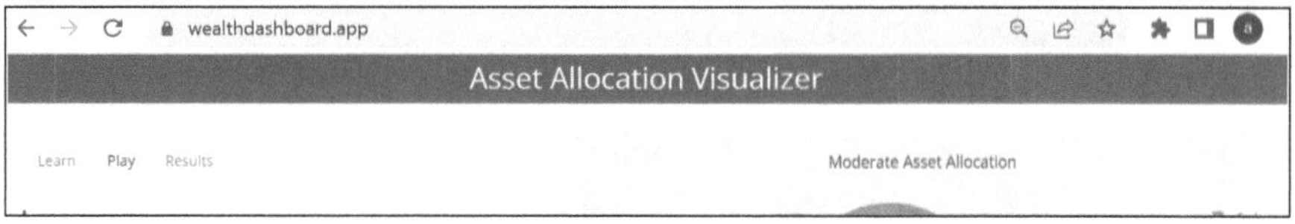

Figure 6-3: Header bar of the Asset Allocation Visualizer app

We style the header using Bootstrap utility classes. We use `text-center` to center the text, `bg-primary` to set the background to the `SPACELAB` theme's primary color, `text-white` to set the text color, and `p-2` to add padding. To see all the Bootstrap utility classes available for styling your app, see the Dash Bootstrap cheat sheet at *https://dashcheatsheet.pythonanywhere.com*.

The second row ❷ has two columns and contains the main content of the app, shown in Figure 6-4. The left column contains the user input control panel tabs. The right column has the primary outputs, which are the pie chart, line chart, and summary table visualizations. There is a lot of information in this row. If the screen were static, someone viewing it on a small screen would have to zoom in and do a lot of scrolling to see the information. The good news is that Bootstrap can easily make our apps responsive to the size of the device being used. We simply set screens that are smaller than tablet size to show just one column at a time, and screens that are larger to show the two columns side by side.

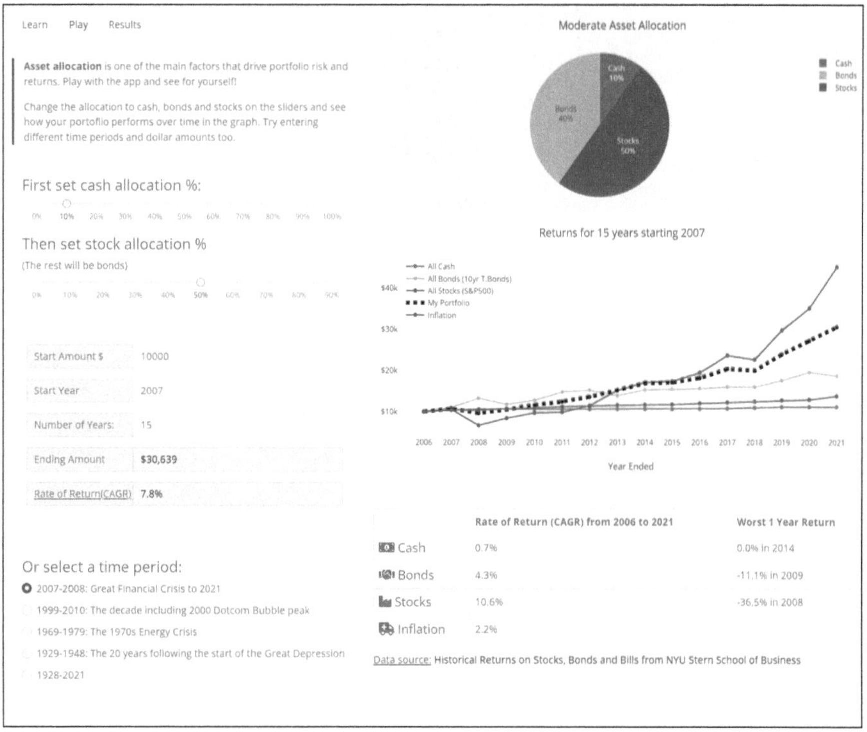

Figure 6-4: The main content of the resultant app

Since Bootstrap rows have 12 columns, we make the row span the full screen by setting the width to 12. Then, on large screens, we set the first column to a width of 5 and the second column to a width of 7 so that they will show side by side. Here is a simplified example:

```
dbc.Row(
    [
        dbc.Col("column 1", width=12, lg=5),
        dbc.Col("column 2", width=12, lg=7)
    ]
)
```

At the bottom we place the footer, shown in Figure 6-5. For consistency, it's styled the same as the header. A website's footer is located at the bottom of every page and commonly includes secondary information such as contact information, legal notices, and a sitemap.

Figure 6-5: The app's footer

Finally, we set the property `fluid=True` ❸. This makes the content span the width of the *viewport*, which is the area of a web page visible to the user and which varies with the device. The viewport is smaller on phones and tablets than on a computer screen, so setting `fluid=True` allows the app to have a responsive design that accommodates this. More on this topic shortly. That's it for the main layout!

Components

Now we'll describe in more detail how to define each component we added to the layout. You'll notice the app has different *tabs* which define different panes for content, such as the tutorial (the Learn tab), the app controls (the Play tab), and the data (the Results tab). If you click between the tabs, you'll see that only the content in the first column changes; the second column, which displays the graphs and summary table, always stays the same when you are just switching tabs.

The Play tab is the busiest, and we'll look over each of the following elements in detail:

- `dcc.Markdown` for formatting and displaying the intro text
- `dbc.Card` and `dcc.Slider` components for setting the asset allocation percentages
- `dbc.Input`, `dbc.InputGroup`, and `dbc.InputGroupText` for making the form for entering the numeric data
- `dbc.Tooltip` for displaying additional data on hover

In the Results tab, we use `DataTable` to display the source data and results for visualization.

Tabs

In Dash, the `Tabs` component provides a convenient way to separate content into different panes. A user can click a tab to view the pane, and the best part is that the component automatically handles this navigation for us. All we need to do is define what content goes in each tab. Figure 6-6 shows the tabs in our app.

| Learn | **Play** | Results |

Figure 6-6: The Asset Allocation Visualizer tabs

The Learn tab has some text. The Play tab is the main control panel for the app, which allows the user to input their choices. The Results tab contains tables with details of the annual returns of the portfolio and the source data. This is the data that's visualized in the second column.

In `app.layout`, we included these tabs by simply including the variable name tabs in the first column of the second row:

```
--snip--
  dbc.Row(
    [
        dbc.Col(tabs, width=12, lg=5, className="mt-4 border"),
--snip--
```

We define our tabs as shown in Listing 6-3.

```
tabs = dbc.Tabs(
  [
    dbc.Tab(learn_card, tab_id="tab1", label="Learn"),
❶ dbc.Tab(
        [asset_allocation_text, slider_card, input_groups,
        time_period_card],
        tab_id="tab-2",
        label="Play",
        className="pb-4",
    ),
    dbc.Tab([results_card, data_source_card],
        tab_id="tab-3", label="Results"),
  ],
  id="tabs",
❷ active_tab="tab-2",
)
```

Listing 6-3: Defining the tabs

We create a `tabs` container with the `dbc.Tabs` component, which holds our three separate Tab panes. We give each `dbc.Tab` the content to display, an ID, and a label that will be displayed on the screen. Take a look at the second `dbc.Tab` ❶, which is the Play tab depicted in Figure 6-7, and you'll see that the `children` property includes a list of variable names that correspond to components we've defined separately in the components section of the code. `asset_allocation_text` contains the text of the introduction. `slider_card` contains the two `dcc.Slider`s where the user can set the allocation percentage between cash, stocks, and bonds. `input_groups` defines the area for entering all user input: the starting dollar amount, number of years, and starting year. We use this input for calculating the investment returns. `time_period_card` allows the user to select certain interesting periods, like the dot-com bubble or the Great Depression.

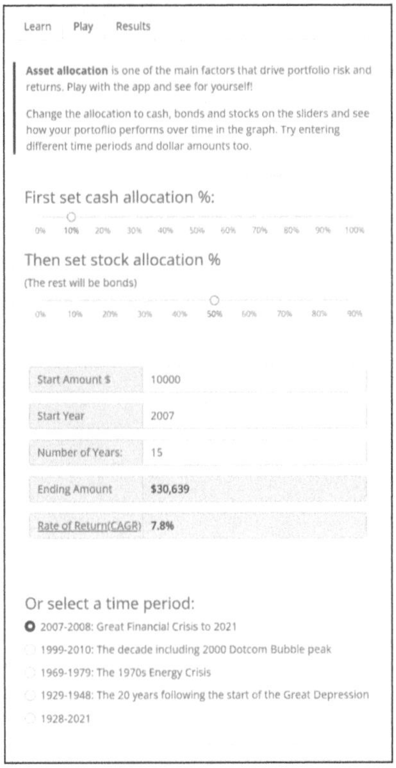

Figure 6-7: The full content of the Play tab

Now try moving the `asset_allocation_text` variable name to the last item in the list. When you run the app with that change, you'll see the intro text is moved to the bottom of the tab screen. This shows how easy it is to make design changes when using this technique for structuring the app. In the next section we'll discuss in more detail how each section is defined.

The `active_tab` property ❷ specifies the default tab to show when the app starts. By setting it to 2, we ensure that the app always opens on the Play tab.

Card Containers and Sliders

A Bootstrap dbc.Card is a convenient container for related content. It's typi-cally a bordered box with padding and has options for headers, footers, and other content. We can also use Bootstrap utility classes to style and position cards easily.

We use dbc.Card in several places in the app, but we'll just examine the code for the card shown in Figure 6-8 as a representative example.

Figure 6-8: An example dbc.Card

Listing 6-4 shows the code for the Card component shown in Figure 6-6.

```
slider_card = dbc.Card(
    [
        html.H4("First set cash allocation %:", className="card-title"),
        dcc.Slider(
            id="cash",
            marks={i: f"{i}%" for i in range(0, 101, 10)},
            min=0,
            max=100,
            step=5,
            value=10,
            included=False,
        ),
        html.H4("Then set stock allocation % ", className="card-title mt-3",),
        html.Div("(The rest will be bonds)", className="card-title"),
        dcc.Slider(
            id="stock_bond",
            marks={i: f"{i}%" for i in range(0, 91, 10)},
            min=0,
            max=90,
            step=5,
            value=50,
            included=False,
        ),
    ],
    body=True,
    className="mt-4",
)
```

Listing 6-4: The allocation slider card

For the slider label, we use the Dash component `html.H4` to set a level 4 heading and the Bootstrap class `card-title` to set consistent spacing for the selected theme.

`dcc.Slider` is a Dash Core component. In Chapter 5 we saw `dcc.RangeSlider`, which allows the user to select the start and end values of a range. `dcc.Slider` is similar, but only allows you to select a single value. We give the slider an id that we can reference in a callback, and we set the initial settings for `marks`, `min`, `max`, `step`, and `value` to select on the slider. These are the defaults you see when the app starts.

The `included` property sets the style of the slider rail. By default, the sections of the slider rail before the slider handle are highlighted. However, for our use we are specifying a discrete value, so it makes sense to only highlight the value and not a range. We do this by setting `included=False`.

Look for other cards in the app and you will see that they are constructed in a similar way but hold different components, such as `dbc.RadioItems`, `dbc.InputGroup`, and `dcc.Markdown`.

Input Containers

The `dbc.Input` component handles user input, and `dbc.InputGroup` is a container that enhances `dbc.Input` with more features, such as icons, text, buttons, and dropdown menus.

Figure 6-9 shows how we use `dbc.InputGroup` in our app to create a form with the variable name input_groups.

Start Amount $	10000
Start Year	2007
Number of Years:	15
Ending Amount	**$30,639**
Rate of Return(CAGR)	**7.8%**

Figure 6-9: Input form

Each line is one `dbc.InputGroup` item, so here we have five items together in one container. In this case, rather than use a `Card` as a container, we use an `html.Div` container, simply because it doesn't have a border and padding by default. Here's the containing `Div`:

```
input_groups = html.Div(
    [start_amount, start_year, number_of_years, end_amount, rate_of_return],
    className="mt-4 p-4",
)
```

We define each `InputGroup` item separately and add it to the `html.Div` container. Each item is quite similar, so we will just look at a couple of them in detail. Here we define the second item, the "Start Year":

```
start_year = dbc.InputGroup(
    [
        dbc.InputGroupText("Start Year"),
        dbc.Input(
            id="start_yr",
            placeholder=f"min {MIN_YR}  max {MAX_YR}",
            type="number",
            min=MIN_YR,
            max=MAX_YR,
            value=START_YR,
        ),
    ],
    className="mb-3",
)
```

You use the `dbc.InputGroupText` component to add text before, after, or on both sides of an input field. This makes forms look more attractive. For example, here we use `dbc.InputGroupText("Start Year")` to display the text "Start Year" before the `dbc.Input`.

We set `min` and `max`, props of `dbc.Input`, to give an accepted range of values, and `type` to only accept numbers; this helps with data validation. For the values for `min` and `max` we use the `MIN_YR` and `MAX_YR` global variables we discussed earlier. The `placeholder` will show helpful information about the valid range if the input field is empty. Because we use our global variables when we update the datafile, we won't have to make any changes to this component for the new date range.

The last two `InputGroup` items are not actually used for input, but rather to show some results. We set `disabled=True` so that nothing can be entered, and we set the background color to gray to differentiate the items. In the callback we'll update this field with the investment results. It may seem odd to use an input component as an output field, but doing it like this gives the group a consistent look. Plus, in the future we may decide to allow input data here. For example, the user could enter the ending dollar amount and see how much would need to be invested, and for how long, to reach that goal in different market conditions. The code for the `rate_of_return` input group looks like this:

```
rate_of_return = dbc.InputGroup(
    [
        dbc.InputGroupText(
            "Rate of Return(CAGR)",
            id="tooltip_target",
            className="text-decoration-underline",
        ),
        dbc.Input(id="cagr", disabled=True, className="text-black"),
```

```
        dbc.Tooltip(cagr_text, target="tooltip_target")
    ],
    className="mb-3",
)
```

Tool Tips

Tool tips are textual hints that appear when the user hovers their mouse over a component, as shown in Figure 6-10. To add them we use the `dbc.Tooltip` component and style it with Bootstrap. You just need to specify the `Tooltip`'s `target id`—no callback required! We use this in the app to provide a definition of CAGR, since it's a term many people are not familiar with. The snippet at the end of the preceding section shows the code for the `Tooltip` in the `rate_of_return` input group.

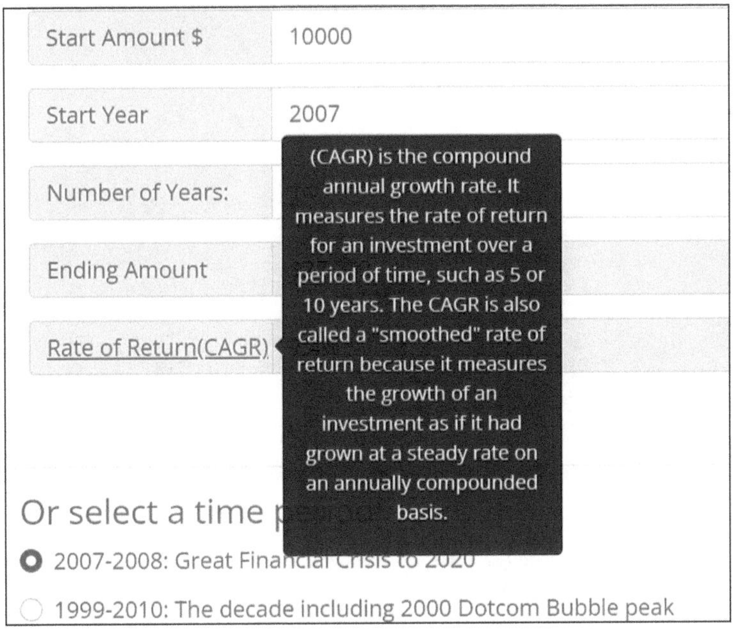

Figure 6-10: Tool tip example

Data Tables

The `DataTable` is an interactive table for viewing, editing, and exploring large datasets. This app uses only a small portion of its capabilities, so be sure to check out the Dash documentation to see more examples of how to use this powerful tool. We use a `DataTable` to show the `total_returns_table` in the Results tab, shown in Figure 6-11.

Learn Play Results

My Portfolio Returns - Rebalanced Annually

Year	Cash	Bonds	Stocks	Total
2006	$1,000	$4,000	$5,000	$10,000
2007	$1,044	$4,408	$5,274	$10,726
2008	$1,087	$5,153	$3,403	$9,643
2009	$966	$3,428	$6,072	$10,466
2010	$1,048	$4,541	$6,009	$11,597
2011	$1,160	$5,383	$5,920	$12,464
2012	$1,247	$5,134	$7,222	$13,603
2013	$1,361	$4,946	$8,988	$15,295
2014	$1,530	$6,776	$8,682	$16,987
2015	$1,700	$6,882	$8,611	$17,193
2016	$1,725	$6,924	$9,608	$18,257
2017	$1,843	$7,507	$11,101	$20,451
2018	$2,085	$8,179	$9,793	$20,057
2019	$2,037	$8,796	$13,159	$23,992
2020	$2,401	$10,684	$14,157	$27,242

Figure 6-11: The full Results tab

Listing 6-5 shows the code for the `DataTable`.

```
total_returns_table = dash_table.DataTable(
   id="total_returns",
   columns=[{"id": "Year", "name": "Year", "type": "text"}]
   + [
        {"id": col, "name": col, "type": "numeric", "format": {"specifier": "$,.0f"}}
        for col in ["Cash", "Bonds", "Stocks", "Total"]
   ],
   page_size=15,
   style_table={"overflowX": "scroll"},
)
```

Listing 6-5: Code for the `DataTable` shown in Figure 6-11

Like other elements in our app, we assign the `DataTable` to a variable to make it easy to call in the layout.

We use the following component properties to define our table:

- The table `id` is `"total_returns"`; we use this to identify this component in a callback.
- The column `id` matches the column name of our pandas DataFrame, which is what we use to update the data in the cells of the table.
- The column `name` is the text displayed in the column header.

- The column type sets the data type to either text or numeric.
- "format": {"specifier": "$,.0f"} formats the cells with a dollar sign ($) and zero (0) decimals so that the data is displayed in whole dollars. Note that the data type must be numeric for the formatting to be applied correctly.
- The page_size prop controls the table height and adds the pagination buttons at the bottom of the table. We set it to 15 to display 15 rows per page. The style_table={"overflowX": "scroll"} syntax controls the width by adding a scroll bar if the table would otherwise overflow the parent container.

Content Tables

The dbc.Table component is a great way to style basic HTML tables with a Bootstrap theme. HTML tables are convenient when you have just a few items to display, and they can contain other Dash components such as dcc.Graph or dbc.Button as content. It's not possible to do that today with a Dash DataTable.

We use a dbc.Table in the app for the summary table shown in Figure 6-12. This allows us to include Dash components and use the FontAwesome icons in the summary table.

	Rate of Return (CAGR) from 2006 to 2021	Worst 1 Year Return
Cash	0.7%	0.0% in 2014
Bonds	4.3%	-11.1% in 2009
Stocks	10.6%	-36.5% in 2008
Inflation	2.2%	

Figure 6-12: Summary table from the Asset Allocation Visualizer app

Listing 6-6 shows a portion of the code, but the big picture is that we create this table with a function.

```
def make_summary_table(dff):
    # Create new dataframe with info to include in the table
    df_table = pd.DataFrame(...)
    return dbc.Table.from_dataframe (df_table, bordered=True, hover=True)
```

Listing 6-6: An excerpt from the summary table code

We'll use this function in a callback later in the chapter. The function argument is a DataFrame created from the user's input. Then we make another DataFrame that contains only the information we want to display in the summary table. We use the dash-bootstrap-components helper function dbc.Table.from_dataframe() to build the HTML table.

Markdown Text

Markdown is a markup language for formatting text for web pages, and it is one of the most popular ways to add and format text with boldface, italics, headers, lists, and more. To learn more about Markdown syntax, check out the tutorial at *https://commonmark.org/help.*

We use the `dcc.Markdown` component to add formatted text to apps. In this app, we use it to add the description of asset allocation shown in Figure 6-13. Markdown syntax uses ** to highlight some text and > to format the text as a blockquote.

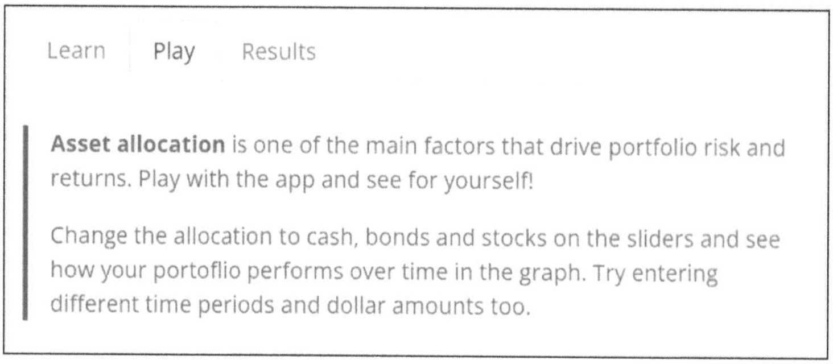

Learn | Play   Results

Asset allocation is one of the main factors that drive portfolio risk and returns. Play with the app and see for yourself!

Change the allocation to cash, bonds and stocks on the sliders and see how your portoflio performs over time in the graph. Try entering different time periods and dollar amounts too.

Figure 6-13: Adding text with Markdown

Here's the code for the `Markdown` component:

```
asset_allocation_text = dcc.Markdown(
    """
> **Asset allocation** is one of the main factors that drive portfolio risk and returns. Play
with the app and see for yourself!
> Change the allocation to cash, bonds and stocks on the sliders and see how your portfolio
performs over time in the graph.
    Try entering different time periods and dollar amounts too.
    """
)
```

We need to take one more step to make the blockquote appear the way it does in the app. A *blockquote* is typically an extended quote from a different source, but it can also be used to repeat or highlight certain content. A blockquote usually has an additional margin or padding, or other formatting to make it stand out, which is why we chose it for this particular situation.

The default style for a blockquote in Bootstrap is:

```
blockquote {
    margin: 0 0 1rem;
}
```

This gives no margin on the top or the right, and just `1rem` on the bottom. (A *rem* is the font size of the root element and is often 16 pixels.) This doesn't really make the text stand out, so we add a little more margin and some color, like so:

```
blockquote {
    border-left: 4px var(--bs-primary) solid;
    padding-left: 1rem;
    margin-top: 2rem;
    margin-bottom: 2rem;
    margin-left: 0rem;
}
```

This adds a left border that is four pixels wide and matches the color to the header and footer. It also adds a little more margin and padding. Here's a CSS trick that comes in handy when you use Bootstrap: instead of specifying a color using a hex number, like #446e9b, you can use a Bootstrap color name, like this: var(--bs-primary). This code will match the color to the Bootstrap theme's "primary" color. If you change the Bootstrap theme in the app, this blockquote's left margin color will update automatically to the primary color of that theme, to keep everything in the app looking consistent.

This custom CSS is saved in a file named *mycss.css* in the *assets* folder. You can name the file anything you like as long as it has the *.css* extension, and Dash will automatically include this custom CSS in the app.

Pie Chart Using Plotly Graph Objects

This is a very brief introduction to creating figures with Plotly Graph Objects, which provides more sophisticated options for creating graphs and charts than the simpler Plotly Express. The app's pie chart, shown in Figure 6-14, updates the asset allocation in real time as the user moves the slider handles.

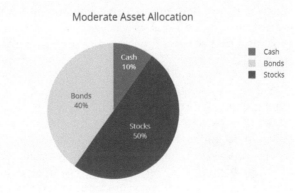

Figure 6-14: Example of a Plotly pie chart

Rather than using Plotly Express to make the figures, like we did in previous chapters, here we use Plotly Graph Objects. Plotly Express preconfigures many of the common parameters so that you can make charts quickly and with less code. However, when you want to do more customization, you may prefer to use Plotly Graph Objects instead. Listing 6-7 shows the code for creating the pie chart.

```
def make_pie(slider_input, title):
    fig = go.Figure(
        data=[
            go.Pie( ❶
                labels=["Cash", "Bonds", "Stocks"],
                values=slider_input,
                textinfo="label+percent",
                textposition="inside",
                marker={"colors": [COLORS["cash"], COLORS["bonds"], COLORS["stocks"]]}, ❷

                sort=False, ❸
                hoverinfo="none",
            )
        ]
    )
    fig.update_layout(
        title_text=title,
        title_x=0.5,
        margin=dict(b=25, t=75, l=35, r=25),
        height=325,
        paper_bgcolor=COLORS["background"],
    )
    return fig
```

Listing 6-7: Creating a Plotly Graph Objects pie chart

To create our pie chart, we start by creating a graph instance with `fig = go.Figure`. The `Figure` syntax here refers to one of the primary classes defined in the `plotly.graph_objects` module (typically imported as `go`), and represents the entire figure. We use this class because instances of the class come bundled with many convenient methods for manipulating their attributes, including `.update.layout()` and `.add.trace()`. In fact, Plotly Express functions use graph objects and return a `plotly.graph_objects.Figure` instance.

The pie chart object in Plotly Graph Objects is `go.Pie` ❶, and it allows us to easily set custom colors for each segment. Note that here we are using the `COLORS` dictionary as a global variable ❷ rather than setting colors for the `marker` directly. This means that if we decide to change the colors later, we only have to update the code in the `COLORS` dictionary and not the code in this figure. In our app we want the color for each asset to stay the same, even if the values change. We do this by setting `sort=False` ❸. (The default is `True` and will sort the values in descending order, so the largest value will always have the same color.)

As with the table in Listing 6-6, we create this pie chart in a function so that we can update it in a callback. The input arguments are the values of the sliders and the title.

Line Chart Using Plotly Graph Objects

We will again use Plotly Graph Objects for our line chart, to allow us to customize the colors and markers for each trace—which would be fairly verbose using Plotly Express.

Again, we create the line chart in a function and input a DataFrame as the argument. This DataFrame is based on user selections: the asset allocation, time period, starting amount, and number of years. You will learn how this DataFrame is created in a callback later in this chapter. Figure 6-15 shows the line chart.

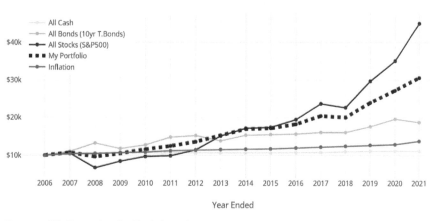

Figure 6-15: Example of a Plotly line chart

Listing 6-8 gives the code for the line chart.

```
def make_line_chart(dff):
    start = dff.loc[1, "Year"]
    yrs = dff["Year"].size - 1
    dtick = 1 if yrs < 16 else 2 if yrs in range(16, 30) else 5

    fig = go.Figure() ❶
    fig.add_trace(
        go.Scatter(
            x=dff["Year"],
            y=dff["all_cash"],
            name="All Cash",
            marker_color=COLORS["cash"],
        )
    )
    fig.add_trace(
        go.Scatter(
            x=dff["Year"],
            y=dff["all_bonds"],
            name="All Bonds (10yr T.Bonds)",
```

```
        marker_color=COLORS["bonds"],
    )
)

# For brevity, the traces for "All Stocks", "My Portfolio", and "Inflation" are excluded

fig.update_layout(
    title=f"Returns for {yrs} years starting {start}",
    template="none",
    showlegend=True,
    legend=dict(x=0.01, y=0.99),
    height=400,
    margin=dict(l=40, r=10, t=60, b=55),
    yaxis=dict(tickprefix="$", fixedrange=True),
    xaxis=dict(title="Year Ended", fixedrange=True, dtick=dtick),
)
return fig
```

Listing 6-8: Creating a Plotly Graph Objects line chart

By using graph_objects we can easily customize each trace (which in this case is a line). We start by creating the figure with fig=go.Figure() ❶, and then add each trace to the chart separately using fig.add_trace(). For this function, the x and y attributes are the data for the x-axis and y-axis of the figure. The x data for every trace is Years and comes from the Year column of the DataFrame. The y data is contained in corresponding columns in the DataFrame. For example, the data for the "All Cash" line is in the DataFrame column dff["all_cash"]. The name attribute will show in the legend and on hover for each trace. The marker_color attribute sets the color of each trace. There are many other attributes for customizing the trace, and you can see them in the Plotly documentation.

We use the fig.update_layout() method to customize the positioning and configuration of the non-data parts of the figure, such as setting the title, height, and margins. The yaxis and xaxis attributes need a little more explanation:

- tickprefix=$ adds a dollar sign to the labels on the y-axis.
- fixedrange=True disables the zoom for both the x-axis and y-axis. This prevents unintended zooming on touchscreens; it can be annoying when you're trying to scroll the page and end up zooming in on the figure instead.
- dtict=dict is used to set the step between the labels on the x-axis. You can see how the labels change when the user selects different time periods. We calculate it like this:

```
dtick = 1 if yrs < 16 else 2 if yrs in range(16, 30) else 5
```

Dash Callbacks

Now comes the fun part. Callbacks make the app interactive. The callback functions are called automatically whenever an input component's property changes. We'll start with a simple callback that updates the pie chart based on the values of the two sliders.

Next we will show how to use State to get data without triggering a callback.

We'll then discuss a callback that synchronizes components by using the same parameters as both inputs and outputs.

Finally, we'll show a callback with many inputs and outputs, and show how to use functions within the callback to make a large callback more manageable.

Interactive Figures

Let's start with the callback that updates the pie chart. Here's the definition:

```
@app.callback(
    Output("allocation_pie_chart", "figure"),
    Input("stock_bond", "value"),
    Input("cash", "value"),
)
```

First we have the Output of the callback, which updates the pie chart by updating the figure property of dcc.Graph. You can find this dcc.Graph in the app.layout:

```
dcc.Graph(id="allocation_pie_chart", className="mb-2")
```

We then define the inputs for the callback, which are the value property of the slider with the id "stock_bond" and the value property of the slider with the id "cash".

Next we have the callback function, shown in Listing 6-9.

```
def update_pie(stocks, cash):
    bonds = 100 - stocks - cash
    slider_input = [cash, bonds, stocks]

    if stocks >= 70:
        investment_style = "Aggressive"
    elif stocks <= 30:
        investment_style = "Conservative"
    else:
        investment_style = "Moderate"
    figure = make_pie(slider_input, investment_style + " Asset Allocation")
    return figure
```

Listing 6-9: The update_pie() callback function

We first calculate the percentage of bonds based on what the user selected for cash and stocks on the slider, using the operation bonds = 100 - stocks - cash.

Next we update the text for the title of the pie chart. Our rule of thumb is that portfolios with more than 70 percent allocated to stocks have an "Aggressive" investment style, portfolios with less than 30 percent allocated to stocks are "Conservative," and everything else is "Moderate." This title is updated dynamically as the user moves the sliders. We pass this title as an attribute to the make_pie() function.

Finally, we create the figure by calling our function make_pie(), defined in Listing 6-7. By using a function to create the figure, we reduce the amount of code contained in the callback and can use the function in other callbacks as well. The result, more readable and maintainable code.

Now you can go back to the app, see how moving the sliders updates the pie chart, and know how this is accomplished.

Callbacks Using State

The second callback synchronizes the two sliders using one-way synchronization: one slider is used to update the value of a different slider. The "cash" slider will update the "stock_bond" slider, but the "stock_bond" slider won't update the "cash" slider. We update the "stock_bond" slider component after the user selects the cash allocation on the "cash" slider:

```
@app.callback(
    Output("stock_bond", "max"),
    Output("stock_bond", "marks"),
    Output("stock_bond", "value"),
    Input("cash", "value"),
❶   State("stock_bond", "value"),
    )
❷ def update_stock_slider(cash, initial_stock_value):
    max_slider = 100 - int(cash)
    stocks = min(max_slider, initial_stock_value)

    # Formats the slider scale
    if max_slider > 50:
        marks_slider = {i: f"{i}%" for i in range(0, max_slider + 1, 10)}
    elif max_slider <= 15:
        marks_slider = {i: f"{i}%" for i in range(0, max_slider + 1, 1)}
    else:
        marks_slider = {i: f"{i}%" for i in range(0, max_slider + 1, 5)}
    return max_slider, marks_slider, stocks
```

We're using State ❶ in the function definition because we need to know the current input value on the slider in order to calculate the new output value. State does not trigger a callback; its purpose is to provide the current value (the state) of the property at the time the callback is triggered.

At ❷ we begin the callback function. When the user selects the cash allocation, we alter the amount that can be allocated to either stocks or bonds. For example, if the user changes cash to 20 percent, stocks can be a maximum of 80 percent, so we need to update the value of the "stock_bond" slider from wherever it's currently at to the new max of 80 percent.

We also update the scale on the slider by updating the marks. Notice how the stock allocation percentage slider scale goes up by tens in the top half of Figure 6-16 and by single digits in the bottom half.

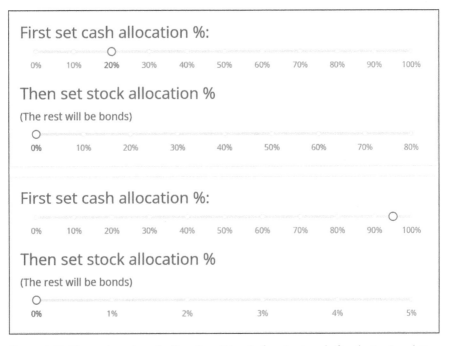

Figure 6-16: The cash and stock allocation sliders before (top) and after (bottom) updating the scale

We calculate the slider marks based on the maximum value of the slider. For example, in the bottom set of sliders, the cash allocation is 95 percent, so the maximum for the stock allocation is 5 percent. This means the max_slider value is 5 in the function that creates the slider marks:

```
marks_slider = {i: f"{i}%" for i in range(0, max_slider + 1)}
```

which is a more compact way of writing it than this:

```
marks_slider={
    0: '0%',
    1: '1%',
    2: '2%',
    3: '3%',
    4: '4%',
    5: '5%'
},
```

Now you can go back to the app and see how moving the "cash" slider updates the "max", "marks", and "value" of the "stock_bond" slider.

Circular Callbacks and Synchronizing Components

Dash also allows two-way synchronization of components. For example, if you would like a user to be able to set a certain value *either* by entering a number into an input box *or* by moving a slider handle, it's necessary to have these values match. In this case, the slider updates the input box and the input box updates the slider. This is an example of a *circular callback*.

We use circular callbacks in our app to synchronize some components in the control panel. Recall that the user can enter a starting year and number of years into input boxes to calculate investment returns, but can also select a certain interesting time period, like the Great Depression, from a list. This callback keeps these three inputs synchronized. When you select the Great Depression from the list, it changes the start year in the input box to 1929 and the planning time to 20 years to highlight how long it took for stocks to recover. If the user then enters 2010 into the input box, it's no longer the Great Depression period, so that radio button is deselected.

Now let's take a closer look at this callback:

```
@app.callback(
    Output("planning_time", "value"),
    Output("start_yr", "value"),
    Output("time_period", "value"),
    Input("planning_time", "value"),
    Input("start_yr", "value"),
    Input("time_period", "value"),
)
```

Notice that under the `@app.callback` decorator function, the three outputs are exactly the same as the three inputs. This makes it possible to synchronize the values of these three components. Listing 6-10 shows the callback function.

```
def update_time_period(planning_time, start_yr, period_number):
    """syncs inputs and selected time periods"""
❶   ctx = callback_context
❷   input_id = ctx.triggered[0]["prop_id"].split(".")[0]

    if input_id == "time_period":
        planning_time = time_period_data[period_number]["planning_time"]
        start_yr = time_period_data[period_number]["start_yr"]

    if input_id in ["planning_time", "start_yr"]:
        period_number = None

    return planning_time, start_yr, period_number
```

Listing 6-10: The callback function for synchronization

To update the output properly, the callback must know which of the three inputs triggered the callback, which we can find out using another advanced callback feature: `callback_context` ❶. This is a global variable that's only available inside a Dash callback. One of the attributes of callback_context is called `triggered` and is a list of changed properties. We parse this list to find the `id` of the triggering input ❷.

Next we use the `input_id` to update different things depending on which input triggered the callback. If it's triggered by the user selecting a time period, we update the input boxes for the year and planning time. If it's triggered by the user entering something in the input boxes, we deselect the time period radio button. This keeps the UI synchronized.

Note that in order to have synced components like this, it's necessary to have the inputs and outputs in the same callback, which we'll cover next.

Callbacks with Multiple Inputs and Multiple Outputs

One of the current limitations of Dash is that it does not allow for multiple callbacks to update the same output. Currently the only available solution is to include all the inputs that update an output in the same callback. The downside to this approach is that the callbacks can become huge and complex, which can make them difficult to understand, maintain, and debug. The strategy to deal with this is to make separate functions for each process in the callback. You can see an example of this in the callback in Listing 6-11.

This callback is the workhorse of the app. Anytime any input changes in the sliders or input boxes, this callback is triggered to update the total returns table, line chart, summary table, ending amount, and rate of return. Wow. If we included the code for all that in this callback it would be hundreds of lines long. Instead, it's 15 lines (not including comments and whitespace). We can make it so concise because we create and call functions that handle the specific changes required. Listing 6-11 shows the full callback.

```
@app.callback(
    Output("total_returns", "data"),
    Output("returns_chart", "figure"),
    Output("summary_table", "children"),
    Output("ending_amount", "value"),
    Output("cagr", "value"),
    Input("stock_bond", "value"),
    Input("cash", "value"),
    Input("starting_amount", "value"),
    Input("planning_time", "value"),
    Input("start_yr", "value"),
)
def update_totals(stocks, cash, start_bal, planning_time, start_yr):
    # Set defaults for invalid inputs
    start_bal = 10 if start_bal is None else start_bal
    planning_time = 1 if planning_time is None else planning_time
    start_yr = MIN_YR if start_yr is None else int(start_yr)

    # Calculate valid planning time start yr
    max_time = MAX_YR + 1 - start_yr
    planning_time = min(max_time, planning_time)
    if start_yr + planning_time > MAX_YR:
        start_yr = min(df.iloc[-planning_time, 0], MAX_YR) # 0 is Year column
```

```
# Create investment returns dataframe
dff = backtest(stocks, cash, start_bal, planning_time, start_yr)

# Create data for DataTable
data = dff.to_dict("records")

fig = make_line_chart(dff) ❶

summary_table = make_summary_table(dff) ❷

# Format ending balance
ending_amount = f"${dff['Total'].iloc[-1]:0,.0f}"

# Calculate cagr
ending_cagr = cagr(dff["Total"])

return data, fig, summary_table, ending_amount, ending_cagr
```

Listing 6-11: The full callback for updating multiple outputs

The lines at ❶ and ❷ are examples of where we use two functions that we described in the "Line Chart Using Plotly Graph Objects" and "Content Tables" sections earlier in the chapter. The first function makes the line chart and the second function makes the summary table. We use the two functions backtest() and cagr() to calculate the investment returns. Those aren't discussed in detail in this chapter, but you can see them in the helper function section in the code on GitHub.

Summary

We'll wrap up this chapter with a summary of the strategies for structuring larger apps:

- Use global variables for constant app data such as thematic app colors and startup defaults.
- Assign variable names to components to make them easier to call in the layout. This also means we use reuse the components in other apps, like building blocks.
- Organize code to keep similar elements together; for example, have discrete sections for visuals such as tables, graphs, and inputs.
- Use functions to bundle logic to make the code easier to read and understand. This is especially useful in callbacks with multiple inputs and outputs.

When developing large apps or adding new features to an existing app, it can be helpful to first create a stand-alone minimal working example of the new feature. This smaller version is much easier to debug, since you don't have to search through hundreds or thousands of lines of code to find the source of the error.

In the next chapter you will learn even more techniques for structuring apps, such as using multiple files and reusable components.

7

EXPLORING MACHINE LEARNING

 This chapter explains how you can use Dash to visually explore and present the internals of machine learning models and classification algorithms. For instance, say you create a machine learning model for self-driving cars that classifies objects into humans, plants, and other cars, and you need to be able to explain to other programmers and non-technical management how and why your model works. Dashboard apps can help you do this in a quick, convincing, and visually appealing way.

In particular, this chapter starts with a conceptual introduction to the *support vector machine (SVM)*, the popular machine learning classification algorithm. SVMs provide a way to categorize data by telling us how to accurately split the data so that it is placed in the correct category. We'll visualize the functioning of SVMs in a dashboard app using various kinds of plots and graphs.

We'll then use the powerful NumPy library for numerical computations and the easy-to-use machine learning algorithms from scikit-learn. Most importantly, you'll experience the great benefit of being able to use the gallery as a basis for diving deeper into more advanced dashboard applications written by the pros.

This chapter also introduces *wrapper functions*, a new Dash concept for creating custom, reusable components to give you more options than just the predefined Dash and HTML components. You'll also learn about some new Dash standard components such as contour plots and graphs, and we'll cover the Dash *load spinner*, which gives the user visual feedback when a specific dashboard component is loading. Load spinners are useful for more complicated dashboard applications that build slowly, often due to heavy computational load.

NOTE   *The purpose of this chapter is to provide you with an overview of what is possible with Dash and to help you develop further skills. We don't go too far into the weeds on any one topic. Our intention is to be informative rather than comprehensive, so if anything is particularly interesting to you, we recommend you check out the supplementary material on the Charming Data YouTube channel and on the companion website to this book:* https://learnplotlydash.com.

Dashboard Apps to Make Machine Learning Models More Intuitive

As machine learning becomes more prevalent in computer science and in our everyday lives, it's increasingly important to understand how computers reach the conclusions they reach. Machines can beat human grandmasters in chess and Go, reduce accident rates in many traffic scenarios, and produce more goods than human workers in a factory environment. When it comes to measurable performance, machines can often prove their superiority, convincing even the fiercest critics that their power can free up human labor.

However, it can be dangerous to observe the effectiveness of machines only through their performance metrics. We can't know how machines will perform in extreme situations that couldn't have been learned from datasets; data-driven approaches will always be biased toward past experiences. If a machine has not observed a stock market crash of 95 percent in 100 years of stock market history, it will unlikely consider this scenario in its models, but this scenario will likely occur someday in the future.

To mitigate this danger, organizations must better understand where the "intelligence" of machines comes from. What are their assumptions? On what basis do they reach their conclusions? How does their behavior change when presented with extreme inputs? A machine learning model from the

1960s would undoubtedly consider negative interest rates as "extreme" or even "impossible." Today we know better.

This leads us to the motivation of machine learning dashboards. A dashboard is a powerful tool for visualizing what is going on *inside* a machine. You can train a model and observe how it performs when given changing inputs. You can test extreme cases. You can see the internals and assess potential risks by overfitting the learning to past data.

Visualizing machine learning models allows you to *show* your models to your clients, enabling them to play with the input parameters and reach a level of trust in the models that would never have been possible in command line models. Dashboards help make the intelligence of your machines tangible.

Classification: A Short Guide

You don't need to have an in-depth understanding of classification or SVMs to follow the app in this chapter. We'll go into some detail to facilitate understanding for those who are interested, but if you want to skip this section and the SVM section after it, feel free to do so and treat the SVM algorithm as a black box as you read through the rest of the chapter.

Still here? Okay, let's dive into the very basics of the classification problem in machine learning.

Generally, the classification problem attempts to assign a category (that is, a class) to input data based on the learnings from a set of provided labeled (classified) training data. For example, if we want to predict what major students will likely study at college based on training data, we might measure aptitude for creative and logical thinking for each student in a school. The goal is to create a classification algorithm that predicts a label—the students' predicted majors—from the features: aptitude for creative versus logical thinking.

SVMs, such as the one visualized in this dashboard app, are *classification* algorithms. Classification algorithms take a set of data and assign to each data point a label corresponding to a particular category, based on model learnings from training data. More specifically, a classification algorithm will search for a *decision boundary* that divides the data into two or more classes. A linear SVM models the decision boundary in an n-dimensional space as an $(n - 1)$-dimensional plane that divides the data points into two classes. All data points on one side of the decision boundary belong to one class and all data points on the other side belong to another class. Thus, assuming you can represent all data points in an n-dimensional space and you have an $(n - 1)$-dimensional decision boundary, you can use the decision boundary to classify new data, because any new data point falls on exactly one side of the boundary. Roughly speaking, the goal of classification, then, is to identify the decision boundary that separates the training and test data well.

Figure 7-1 gives an example inspired by but slightly modified from *Python One-Liners* by Christian Mayer (No Starch Press, 2020).

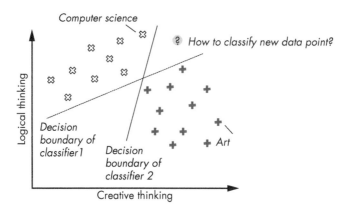

Figure 7-1: Example classification problem: different decision boundaries would lead to different classifications of the new data point (either "computer science" or "art")

This classification scenario creates a classification model that helps aspiring university students find a field of study that may fit their strengths. We have training data from previous students from two fields: computer science and art. Fortunately, the students already provided us with an estimation of their own logical and creative thinking skills. When mapped into a two-dimensional space that models logical and creative thinking as separate axes, the data seems to be clustered so that the computer science students tend to be strong in logical thinking whereas the artists tend to be strong in creative thinking. We use the data to find a decision boundary that maximizes the classification accuracy for the training data. Technically, the obtained classification model will only give aspiring students a hint about what they are likely to pick based on their strengths. It doesn't necessarily help them decide what they should be picking (for example, to maximize their happiness). That is a much harder problem.

We'll use the decision boundary to classify new users for whom we only have data on their logic and creativity. The figure shows two linear classifiers (depicted with lines) that perfectly separate the data when used as decision boundaries. They have 100 percent accuracy when classifying the test data, so both lines seem to be equally good. For a machine learning algorithm to perform well, it must choose the decision boundary wisely. But how do we find the best one?

Support Vector Machines

SVMs attempt to maximize the distance between the closest data points from both classes and the decision boundary; this distance between the closest points and the decision boundary line is known as the *margin of safety*, *safety margin*, or just *margin*. These closest data points are called *support vectors*. By maximizing the margin of safety, SVMs aim to minimize the error when classifying new points that are close to the decision boundary.

As a visual example, take a look at Figure 7-2.

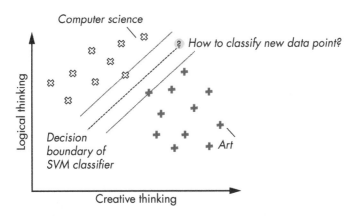

Figure 7-2: Example SVM classification with decision boundary and support vectors

The SVM classifier finds the support vectors for each class and places the line at the greatest distance from each (halfway between) so that the zone between the different support vectors is as thick as possible. This line is the decision boundary. In Figure 7-2 a new data point is added that needs classifying; however, because the point to be classified falls in the margin zone, the model cannot confidently decide whether it belongs to the art class or the computer science class. This nicely demonstrates that SVMs come with a built-in mechanism to explicitly tell us whether the model performs a borderline classification. For example, the SVM may tell us that a student ranking high on creativity belongs to the art class and a student ranking high in logical thinking belongs to the computer science class, but a student ranking high in creativity *and* logic cannot be confidently assigned to either class.

Note that SVM models can also be trained in a way that allows for *outliers* in the training data; these are points that fall on one side of the decision boundary but belong to the other side. This is the most common case for real-world data. However, instead of exploring these SVM optimizations further, we suggest you check out the excellent SVM classification tutorials listed at the end of this chapter so that we can dive into the exciting dashboard app right away.

The SVM Explorer App

Figure 7-3 shows how we can visualize SVMs using the SVM Explorer app, a Python dashboard app from the gallery that uses various kinds of plots and graphs. Feel free to play with the live project at *https://dash-gallery.plotly.host/dash-svm*.

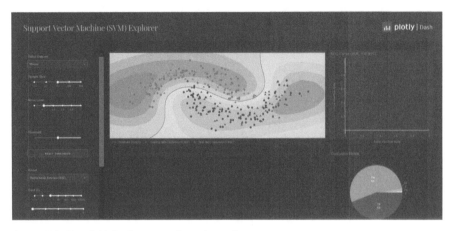

Figure 7-3: The SVM Explorer app from the gallery

We'll give you an overview of the SVM Explorer app first so that you can gain a rough understanding. The app showcases how a given SVM model classifies a given training dataset. You control the model using the dashboard controls, such as sliders, dropdowns, and radio buttons. Based on your selections, the output graphs and plots change to reflect the changing instantiation of the SVM model.

One of the authors of this app, Xing Han, has kindly provided us with a quick overview of the SVM Explorer app:

> This app is fully written in Dash and scikit-learn. All the components are used as input parameters for scikit-learn functions, which then generate a model with respect to the parameters the user changes. The model then performs predictions that are displayed on a contour plot, and its predictions are evaluated to create the ROC [receiver operating characteristic] curve and confusion matrix. In addition to creating models, it uses scikit-learn to generate the datasets you see, as well as the data needed for the metrics plots.

Let's quickly examine each visible component. There are multiple input components in the left column of the dashboard:

- The *Select Dataset* dropdown menu allows you to choose the synthetic dataset to use for training and testing. The default selection is Moon, named for its moon-shaped dataset. This input dropdown allows you to explore how the SVM model works on data with different inherent properties. For example, you can select the Circles dataset (not shown in the figure), which is nonlinear, so that the two datasets to be classified are shaped like an inner circle and an outer ring around that circle. The SVM model can classify those types of data too!
- The *Sample Size* slider allows you to control the number of data points used to test and train the model. A higher sample size usually leads to a more accurate model, which is why machine learning companies never

stop collecting more data! In our toy dashboard, however, a higher sample size may result in a more crowded visualization.

- The *Noise Level* slider allows you to control the standard deviation of Gaussian noise added to the data. A higher noise level yields a less accurate model because noise reduces the clarity of patterns in the data and makes it harder to find a separating decision boundary during the training phase. You can, however, use the Noise Level slider to check how robust the SVM model will be in practice, because real-world data tends to be noisy.

- The *Threshold* slider allows you to add a bias toward one class or the other. Roughly speaking, by increasing the threshold value you shift the decision boundary from class A more toward class B (or vice versa by decreasing the threshold) so that for a given input, the likelihood of being classified as A increases. For example, if the threshold is 0.4, any score greater than 0.4 is considered a positive prediction and any score less than 0.4 is considered a negative prediction on whether the point belongs to a certain class.

- The *Reset Threshold* button resets the threshold to a default value without a customized threshold or bias.

- The *Kernel* dropdown menu, the *Costs* sliders, and other controls such as the *Gamma* slider and the *Shrinking* radio buttons allow you to further control other SVM parameters and their effect on classification accuracy. Discussing these parameters would need more than just one or two sentences in this quick overview, so we'll skip it. If you're interested in learning the theory behind these controls, feel free to consult Chapter 15 of *Introduction to Information Retrieval* (Cambridge University Press, 2008). You can read the chapter for free at *https://nlp.stanford.edu/IR-book/pdf/15svm.pdf.*

Three output components change as the model changes:

- The *Dash Graph component* is a contour plot that visualizes the training and testing data, as well as the model classification confidence levels, in a heat map overlay. The dots represent the training data and the triangles represent the test data. Red data points belong to one class and blue to another. First we train the SVM model based on a subset of the sample data. Then we classify the test data using the trained model and plot the predicted class in the visualization.

- The *ROC curve plot* is a measure of quality of the SVM model on the given dataset. It measures the *true positive rate*, which is the proportion of data points that are correctly classified, against the *false positive rate*, which is the proportion of data points that are incorrectly classified.

- The *confusion matrix* refers to the predicted versus actual classes. Specifically, it's a bar chart that shows the number of true positive, true negative, false positive, and false negative classifications of the test data. You can think of this as yet another measure of how well the SVM model performs the training and classification task on the given dataset.

We've provided links to more detailed explanations of the Dash Graph, the ROC curve plot, and the confusion matrix at the end of this chapter. However, a great way to get a better understanding is to play around with the SVM Explorer app. We recommend spending 10 to 20 minutes playing with the app to fully grasp the idea of each component.

You can find the code for the app in the GitHub repository at *https:// github.com/DashBookProject/Plotly-Dash/tree/master/Chapter-7*. The complete code has more than 650 lines, but don't worry, we will focus only on the most important aspects. Note that well-maintained code seldom stays the same forever. Since this chapter's writing, the authors have already updated the original code base by adding new styles to the app, among other things. But because the core of the app didn't change, we have provided the original code on the specified GitHub repository so you can download it and reproduce the exact app explained in this chapter. We highly recommend that you download the code to accelerate your learning.

Without further ado, let's dive into the code!

Python Libraries

We'll stand on the shoulders of giants and rely on several Python libraries to create our SVM dashboard app. Listing 7-1 shows the libraries used in this project.

```
import time
import importlib

from dash import Dash, dcc, html, Input, Output, State
import numpy as np
from dash.dependencies import Input, Output, State
❶ from sklearn.model_selection import train_test_split
from sklearn.preprocessing import StandardScaler
from sklearn import datasets
from sklearn.svm import SVC
```

Listing 7-1: Dependencies for the SVM app

You've already seen the Dash library statements that import the core and HTML components, as well as the overall Dash app functionality. The core code in this chapter consists of the computations for the SVM. We won't implement our own SVM from scratch, but we will rely on the excellent implementations provided by the scikit-learn library. We therefore import some modules from this library, which we'll look at in more detail as they come up ❶. If you're interested in machine learning, scikit-learn is your best friend!

Data Management

scikit-learn provides some great synthetic datasets for testing all kinds of classification and prediction algorithms. In Listing 7-2 we show how the function generate_data() dynamically creates the dataset using the number of sample points, the type of the dataset, and the noise level, all specified in the left column of the SVM Explorer app shown in Figure 7-3. We'll use the functions datasets.make_moons(), datasets.make_circles(), and datasets .make_classification() to generate different datasets ("moons", "circles", and "linear", respectively) according to the value obtained through the input dropdown menu. This dataset is used later to train and test our SVM.

```
def generate_data(n_samples, dataset, noise):
    if dataset == "moons":
        return datasets.make_moons(n_samples=n_samples,
                                noise=noise, random_state=0)

    elif dataset == "circles":
        return datasets.make_circles(
            n_samples=n_samples, noise=noise, factor=0.5, random_state=1
        )

    elif dataset == "linear":
        X, y = datasets.make_classification(
            n_samples=n_samples,
            n_features=2,
            n_redundant=0,
            n_informative=2,
            random_state=2,
            n_clusters_per_class=1,
        )

        rng = np.random.RandomState(2)
        X += noise * rng.uniform(size=X.shape)
        linearly_separable = (X, y)

        return linearly_separable

    else:
        raise ValueError(
            "Data type incorrectly specified. Choose an existing dataset."
        )
```

Listing 7-2: Data management for the SVM app

At a high level, the code consists of if...elif...elif...else statements that differentiate user inputs. This allows the user to choose among three datasets: "moons", "circles", and "linear". In each case, a new dataset is created with scikit-learn's dataset.make_X() function, which takes different input arguments (such as the number of sample points) and returns the data as a NumPy array. Interested readers can learn more about the input arguments we used here at *https://scikit-learn.org/stable/modules/classes.html#module-sklearn.datasets*.

Layout and Styling

The layout and styling sections give you an idea of the structure of the SVM Explorer app and the basic Dash components from which it is built. Let's start with the overall layout of the project.

Layout

As you start working on larger apps, the number of lines of code in the *app.py* file quickly becomes harder to manage. To help manage the code, the SVM Explorer app includes a *utils* folder with two helper modules, *dash_resuable_components.py* and *figures.py*, which contain the definitions of some customized Dash components that we'll explore in more detail later in this chapter, as well as some plotting and styling functionality. This approach of pulling out utility functionality from the *app.py* file into some imported external modules is good practice for your own larger dashboard projects, to make sure the main *app.py* remains clean and focused.

The structure of the SVM Explorer app looks like this:

```
- app.py
- utils/
   |--dash_reusable_components.py
   |--figures.py
```

The layout of the app is a hierarchically nested structure of HTML elements, as shown in Listing 7-3.

```
app.layout = html.Div(
   children=[html.Div(...), # Heading etc.
      html.Div(...)] # Body
)
```

Listing 7-3: Zooming one level in the SVM app layout

The first child of the outer `Div` contains the app's heading, logo, and other meta-information. The second child contains the body of the app, which is the central part of the app. Listing 7-4 shows the full code for the layout section of our SVM Explorer app. Just skim over it and try to understand how the app is structured; we'll discuss the relevant parts afterward.

```
❶ app.layout = html.Div(
   children=[
      # .container class is fixed, .container.scalable is scalable
   ❷ html.Div(
         className="banner",
         children=[
            html.Div(
               className="container scalable",
               children=[
                  # Change App Name here
                  html.H2(
                     id="banner-title",
                     children=[
                        html.A(
                           "Support Vector Machine (SVM) Explorer",
                           href=("https://github.com/"
                              "plotly/dash-svm"),
```

```
                            style={
                                "text-decoration": "none",
                                "color": "inherit",
                            },
                        )
                    ],
                ),
                html.A(
                    id="banner-logo",
                    children=[
                        html.Img(src=app.get_asset_url(
                            "dash-logo-new.png"))
                    ],
                    href="https://plot.ly/products/dash/",
                ),
            ],
        )
    ],
),
❸ html.Div(
    id="body",
    className="container scalable",
    children=[
        html.Div(
            id="app-container",
            # className="row",
            children=[
                html.Div(
                    # className="three columns",
                    id="left-column",
                    children=[
# ... See Dash Components
                    ],
                ),
                html.Div(
                    id="div-graphs",
                    children=dcc.Graph(
                        id="graph-sklearn-svm",
                        figure=dict(
                            layout=dict(
                                plot_bgcolor="#282b38",
                                paper_bgcolor="#282b38"
                            )
                        ),
                    ),
                ),
            ],
        )
    ],
),
]
)
```

Listing 7-4: Zooming multiple levels in the SVM app layout

The code references stylesheets and Dash components that we'll talk about in upcoming sections, so it may not be clear how this section works just yet. But it does show you what a nontrivial Dash app looks like: hierarchically nested HTML components using dash-html-components. In large apps you'll use this structure to add more components as you modify the app's look and feel.

As with the smaller apps we've seen in earlier chapters, the app consists of an outer Div ❶ that contains two inner Div elements at ❷ and ❸. The first inner Div contains meta-information, such as the headline and logo. The second inner Div contains the body of the app.

In "Reusable Components" later in this chapter, we'll focus on the different Dash components to learn how they are working individually.

Next, we'll look at the CSS stylesheets we used to style the SVM Explorer app.

Styling

We know from Chapters 4 and 5 that we can style our HTML elements using either a CSS stylesheet or dash-bootstrap-components. In this app we opt for the CSS stylesheet, since it allows us to create a more customized look and feel with margins, padding, colors, fonts, and borders. Note that the main styling is already built into the default Plotly Dash components, so using custom stylesheets is a relatively minor design decision by the creators of the SVM Explorer app.

We define the stylesheet in the *assets* subfolder, with a structure like this:

```
- app.py
- assets/
  |--base-styles.css
  |--custom-styles.css
--snip--
```

We'll use two stylesheets: the *base-styles.css* and *custom-styles.css* files that were added to the SVM Explorer app by the app creators. The *base-styles.css* stylesheet defines how basic HTML elements such as headings and paragraphs should be styled. The *custom-styles.css* stylesheet defines how Dash-specific elements such as named sliders, graph containers, and cards should be styled. Let's quickly dip into *base-styles.css* to see how we can manipulate the default styling.

The *base-styles.css* stylesheet consists of the 13 sections shown in Listing 7-5, each defining how certain types of HTML elements look.

```
/* Table of contents
  ───────────────────
- Grid
- Base Styles
- Typography
- Links
- Buttons
- Forms
```

```
      - Lists
      - Code
      - Tables
      - Spacing
      - Utilities
      - Clearing
      - Media Queries
*/
```

Listing 7-5: Overview of base-styles.css

This stylesheet allows you to define things like the fonts, background colors, margins, and padding for these basic elements. For example, in the typography section, shown in Listing 7-6, we define the font size, weight, and spacing for the different headings.

```
/* Typography
──────────────────*/
h1, h2, h3, h4, h5, h6 {
   margin-top: 0;
   margin-bottom: 0;
   font-weight: 300; }
h1 { font-size: 4.5rem; line-height: 1.2; letter-spacing: -.1rem; margin-bottom: 2rem; }
h2 { font-size: 3.6rem; line-height: 1.25; letter-spacing: -.1rem; margin-bottom: 1.8rem;
margin-top: 1.8rem;}
h3 { font-size: 3.0rem; line-height: 1.3; letter-spacing: -.1rem; margin-bottom: 1.5rem;
margin-top: 1.5rem;}
h4 { font-size: 2.6rem; line-height: 1.35; letter-spacing: -.08rem; margin-bottom: 1.2rem;
margin-top: 1.2rem;}
h5 { font-size: 2.2rem; line-height: 1.5; letter-spacing: -.05rem; margin-bottom: 0.6rem;
margin-top: 0.6rem;}
h6 { font-size: 2.0rem; line-height: 1.6; letter-spacing: 0; margin-bottom: 0.75rem;
margin-top: 0.75rem;}

p {
   margin-top: 0; }
```

Listing 7-6: Zooming into the typography section of base-styles.css

You can see that we set the font size for the top-level heading h1 at 4.5rem so that it's the largest.

We won't go into the specifics of each element in this chapter, though we do recommend that you take a quick look at the code to see how we apply custom styles to various elements.

Instead of losing ourselves in minor CSS details (which you could decide to ignore in your own dashboard app and default to the Dash standard styling), let's have a look at the heart of the SVM app: the Dash components.

Reusable Components

Here we'll look at a new Dash concept in the form of *reusable components,* which allow you to add your own style and functionality to existing components. We use several components in our SVM Explorer app that are similar in pattern to the built-in components but with slight differences, such as dropdown menus with different labels and value ranges. We define the components in the *dash_reusable_components.py* file and instantiate the components with their custom features in *app.py*. First we'll add the *dash _reusable_components.py* module to the *utils* folder:

```
- app.py
- assets/
- utils/
   |--dash_reusable_components.py
--snip--
```

Say our goal is to create a custom button we'll use several times throughout the code. The custom button component could be arbitrarily complex; it might just contain a button label or it might have something more complex, like a chart showing how often the button was clicked over time (yes, Dash can do that!). We want to avoid creating the customized button repeatedly in our *app.py* file for clarity and conciseness. To accomplish this, we create this customized button as an instance of the custom class CustomButton. We define the class in the *dash_reusable_components.py* module once and then can instantiate the customized button component as many times as we like in the main *app.py* file, each potentially with its own individual features, such as different background colors or text.

Defining a Card

In Chapter 6 we used a Bootstrap Card to create a small contained area for content. Here we'll create a Card with multiple components: a label, a slider, and a button. You can think of a Card as a meta component consisting of multiple child components, using a specific (relative) width and padding and adding a solid gray border at the bottom to group the components visually. A Card is actually a wrapper around the HTML component html.Section, a container that groups different HTML elements or text inside a (possibly) styled area. All content in a Section belongs together semantically or thematically. Figure 7-4 gives an example of a Card in our SVM Explorer app that uses the html.Section element to group three components: a label, a slider, and a button.

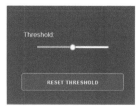

Figure 7-4: Example of a custom Card

Listing 7-7 shows the actual definition of the `Card` wrapper function from *dash_reusable_components.py*.

```
def Card(children, **kwargs):
    return html.Section(className="card", children=children, **_omit(["style"], kwargs))
```

Listing 7-7: Defining the `Card` component

To see how the `Card` component works in full, let's dive deeper into these arguments:

children   A list of other Dash elements that are included in the `Card`, and so are displayed grouped together in the dashboard app. You can create all kinds of nested and hierarchical HTML trees and pass any iterable of HTML elements into the `Card`. The `Card` will then wrap these elements into one common element that resembles a physical card: a 2D box with consistent styling that encloses some other design elements.

**kwargs   Stands for *arbitrary keyword arguments*. The **kwargs argument packs all keyword arguments passed into the function call into a single kwargs dictionary. The keyword argument names are the dictionary keys, and the keyword arguments' values are the dictionary values. For example, if somebody called the function `Card(children, example = "123")`, we could use kwargs['example'] within the function to obtain the value "123". We could use this dictionary later to unpack a potentially large number of arguments into the `html.Section()` constructor, including metadata such as the language of the section or the number of times this component has been clicked by the user. We don't really use the opportunity to pass arbitrary keyword arguments in our SVM Explorer app, but this is an interesting aspect of the `Card` component. You can find a detailed tutorial on the double-asterisk operator at *https://blog.finxter.com/ python-double-asterisk*.

The other argument is actually a function. Let's have a closer look at it:

_omit   Allows us to exclude certain elements if they're not needed. We might, for example, remove the "style" key from the dictionary because it is not needed in the html.Section() constructor, since we already defined the style using the CSS stylesheet. The _omit() function takes two arguments: a list of strings in the variable omitted _keys and a dictionary d. The function returns a new dictionary that consists of the elements in the original dictionary d with all keys in omitted_keys and their associated values filtered out. Here is how the authors of the SVM Explorer app concisely accomplished this:

```
def _omit(omitted_keys, d):
  return {k: v for k, v in d.items() if k not in omitted_keys}
```

In the SVM Explorer app, you call **_omit(["style"], kwargs) to pass the keyword arguments dictionary kwargs from the Card() call after removing the key "style" using the _omit() function. The double-asterisk prefix unpacks all those values from the dictionary into the argument list of the html.Section() constructor.

In *app.py*, we can now use the Card reusable component to create a card containing a named slider and a button, as shown in Listing 7-8.

```
.drc.Card(
    id="button-card",
    children=[
        drc.NamedSlider(
            name="Threshold",
            id="slider-threshold",
            min=0,
            max=1,
            value=0.5,
            step=0.01,
        ),
        html.Button(
            "Reset Threshold",
            id="button-zero-threshold",
        ),
    ],
)
```

Listing 7-8: Combining the named slider and button components within the Card definition

Note that drc.NamedSlider is a reusable component itself, so we wrap a reusable component drc.Card around another reusable component hierarchically.

Figure 7-4 shows how the drc.Card looks in the SVM Explorer app. The named slider consists of two components: an HTML component to display the text "Threshold" and a Dash Slider component to set the float value between 0 and 1.

The threshold is later used as an input value for our SVM model as a means to control the bias of the classification model toward one class or the other. While this is a specific parameter in a specific classification model, you can use this exact strategy to display the performance impact of various model parameters in machine learning. Exploring the impact of a critical parameter becomes as simple as using a slider on your smartphone! Won't this make a lasting impression when you present your next machine learning model to the public?

Now you know how to create reusable components using a wrapper function around another component. Don't worry if you didn't get all the details; we only want you to grasp the big picture: how to create reusable components by means of wrapper functions. Let's dive into the next custom-defined component used in our app: the formatted slider.

Defining a Formatted Slider

The formatted slider is another custom wrapper that consists of an HTML Div element and a dcc.Slider, a Dash Core component introduced in Chapter 6. A formatted slider is a dcc.Slider component with some predefined formatting applied, usually pertaining to padding. For simpler usage, we'd instead use simple CSS to associate formatting with a slider component, but the authors of this app probably considered adding some more advanced components or functionality later, so they made this a reusable component that is easily extendable.

Listing 7-9 shows the code of the wrapper function we place in *dash _reusable_components.py*.

```
def FormattedSlider(**kwargs):
    return html.Div(
        style=kwargs.get("style", {}),
        children=dcc.Slider(**_omit(["style"], kwargs))
    )
```

Listing 7-9: Defining the FormattedSlider component

In *app.py* we create a particular instance of a formatted slider, presented in Figure 7-5, with this slider creation code snippet:

```
drc.FormattedSlider(
    id="slider-svm-parameter-C-coef",
    min=1,
    max=9,
    value=1,
)
```

This creates a formatted slider with a minimum value of 1, a maximum value of 9, and a slider granularity of 1 between two consecutive values. We pass four keyword arguments into the FormattedSlider() function, which are then packed into the kwargs dictionary. There's no style key in the dictionary, so the `kwargs.get("style", {})` call from Listing 7-9 returns the empty dictionary. In this case, the default styling from Dash is used. We pass the remaining key-value pairs in the dictionary as keyword arguments into the `dcc.Slider()` creation routine. These arguments build a new slider with the specified range; note that Dash automatically adds the labels 1, 3, 5, 7, and 9 as values of the specific formatted slider shown in the SVM Explorer app (see Figure 7-5). If you try out the slider yourself, you'll realize that the slider granularity is 1 even though the marks show only every other value. Of course, you can customize the marks if needed by adding another `marks` argument that maps slider values to text labels in a dictionary.

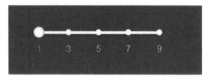

Figure 7-5: Example of a formatted slider

Defining a Named Slider

The named slider is another wrapper around the `dcc.Slider` component that adds a custom heading. Figure 7-6 shows a slider in our SVM Explorer app that we named Degree.

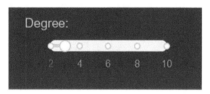

Figure 7-6: Example of a named slider

The code that defines the `NamedSlider` in *dash_reusable_components.py* is shown in Listing 7-10.

```
def NamedSlider(name, **kwargs):
    return html.Div(
        style={"padding": "20px 10px 25px 4px"},
        children=[
            html.P(f"{name}:"),
            html.Div(style={"margin-left": "6px"},
                children=dcc.Slider(**kwargs)),
        ],
    )
```

Listing 7-10: Defining the `NamedSlider` component

We create an HTML `Div` container that contains two elements: an HTML paragraph element that adds the label to the named slider using `html.P()` and another `Div` that contains a regular Dash `dcc.Slider()` element. Here we hardcode some style elements by setting the `padding` attribute of the style dictionary of the outer `Div`. This is a great example of why we might choose to remove the `style` key from the dictionary using _omit(), as discussed earlier; if we wanted to change the style, we'd use this specific style parameter of Dash's HTML components. In our case, the custom styling extends the box width around the named slider component. If we were to change this in *dash_reusable_components.py*, every instance we create in *app.py* would change to match!

We use the formatting string f"{name}:" to access the value of the `name` argument of the `NamedSlider()` call from *app.py* and put it into the string that will serve as the label for our slider. This is what allows us to give each slider its own label.

The `"margin-left"` attribute of the inner `Div` shifts the whole slider slightly to the right to give the appearance of an indentation of the slider component.

NOTE   *The custom function names in* dash_reusable_components.py *start with a capitalized letter by convention because Dash components are capitalized too. This way, calling a reusable component feels similar to calling a predefined Dash component.*

Listing 7-11 shows the code in *app.py* that instantiates the named slider in Figure 7-6.

```
drc.NamedSlider(
    name="Degree",
    id="slider-svm-parameter-degree",
    min=2,
    max=10,
    value=3,
    step=1,
    marks={
        str(i): str(i) for i in range(2, 11, 2)
    },
)
```

Listing 7-11: Instantiating the NamedSlider component

The slider has a minimum value of 2 and a maximum value of 10. We also set the marks of the slider to the integers 2, 4, 6, 8, and 10, created by the generator expression str(i) for i in range(2, 11, 2).

Defining a Named Dropdown

As with the `Slider`, we'll build on `dcc.Dropdown()` to create a named dropdown that includes a label. The process here is similar to creating a named slider, so we'll go over it very briefly to show it to you in different contexts. Listing 7-12 shows the definition that goes in *dash_reusable_components.py*.

```
def NamedDropdown(name, **kwargs):
    return html.Div(
        style={"margin": "10px 0px"},
        children=[
            html.P(children=f"{name}:", style={"margin-left": "3px"}),
            dcc.Dropdown(**kwargs),
        ],
    )
```

Listing 7-12: Defining the NamedDropdown component

We pass through the list of keyword arguments using the double-asterisk operator to both catch all keyword arguments in the kwargs dictionary and unpack all those keyword arguments into the dcc.Dropdown() creation routine. The function argument name that is passed in when creating the NamedDropdown instance serves as the text label in the HTML paragraph element.

The resultant NamedDropdown reusable component will look something like Figure 7-7.

Figure 7-7: Example of a named dropdown

In Listing 7-13 we create this component in *app.py*.

```
drc.NamedDropdown(
    name="Select Dataset",
    id="dropdown-select-dataset",
    options=[
        {"label": "Moons", "value": "moons"},
        {
            "label": "Linearly Separable",
            "value": "linear",
        },
        {
            "label": "Circles",
            "value": "circles",
        },
    ],
    clearable=False,
    searchable=False,
    value="moons",
)
```

Listing 7-13: Instantiating the NamedDropdown component

We call the newly created `drc.NamedDropdown()` function with the name we want to give the named dropdown component. The remaining keyword arguments `id` (identifier of the HTML element), `options` (labels and values of the dropdown), `clearable` (a Boolean either allowing or disallowing users to clear the current selected entry by clicking a small icon), `searchable` (a Boolean either allowing or disallowing users to search the dropdown for a specific value), and `value` (a default dropdown value) are packed into the `kwargs` dictionary and handed downstream to the `dcc.Dropdown()` creation routine.

This instantiation will create the named dropdown in Figure 7-8, with the default dataset set to "Moons" and both `searchable` and `clearable` disabled.

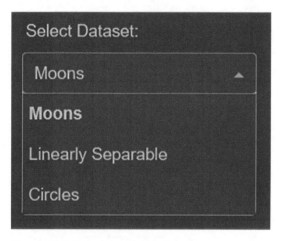

Figure 7-8: Named dropdown clicked state

Using reusable components is an extremely efficient way to scale your application and create whole new libraries for global use. Just define your own *dash_reusable_components.py* file and use the wrapper functions around existing Dash and HTML components in your main program file. Reusable components give you easy ways to customize the look and feel of your app and make your code easier to understand, more concise, and easier to maintain, even if your app requires thousands of lines of code!

Next, we'll dive into some new Dash components in the SVM Explorer app that haven't been covered yet.

Using a Dash Graph

The core component of the whole SVM Explorer app is, of course, the graph that visualizes the learning and classification performance on the chosen training data. Figure 7-9 shows the final graph.

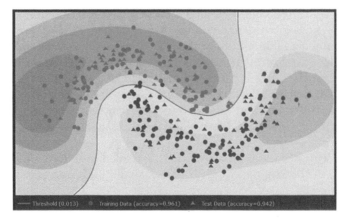

Figure 7-9: Example Dash graph

First we train the model using the input parameters from the different controls in the dashboard. Then we test the accuracy of the model for the test dataset. The dots visualize the training data. The triangles visualize the test data. Red data points belong to one class and blue to another; we'll call them class X and class Y, respectively. For each piece of training data, we already know whether it is X or Y; that is, whether it falls on one side of the decision boundary or the other. The model then estimates which class each piece of test data belongs to, based on the learned decision boundary from the training data.

The following function call accomplishes this powerful visualization (line 434 in the *app.py* sample project):

```
dcc.Graph(id="graph-sklearn-svm", figure=prediction_figure)
```

We create a dcc.Graph component with the id "graph-sklearn-svm". As a figure argument, we pass the prediction_figure variable, which we defined in lines 410 through 421 in *app.py* (see Listing 7-14).

```
prediction_figure = figs.serve_prediction_plot(
    model=clf,
    X_train=X_train,
    X_test=X_test,
    y_train=y_train,
    y_test=y_test,
    Z=Z,
    xx=xx,
    yy=yy,
    mesh_step=h,
    threshold=threshold,
)
```

Listing 7-14: Defining the graph's attributes

We won't go into a lot of technical detail here, but notice that the function call uses four primary datasets: X_train and y_train, as well as X_test and y_test. Like in all supervised learning, we train the model using a training dataset consisting of a collection of *(X, y)* tuples for input data *X* and output data *y* to obtain the mapping $X \rightarrow y$. We pass all these bits of information into the following function:

```
figs.serve_prediction_plot()
```

This function plots the prediction contour of the SVM, the threshold line, and the test and training scatter data. Then it returns the resultant figure as an object that can be passed in the dcc.Graph component, as shown before. We'll break it down and discuss its composite parts. First, the figs section refers to this import statement in the header of *app.py*:

```
import utils.figures as figs
```

We import the figures module from the *utils* folder and name it figs. The module contains utility functions to create the various plots shown in the dashboard, including the serve_prediction_plot() function for the SVM model's training and testing data visualization.

The function serve_prediction_plot() creates the Plotly graph object used to visualize the training and testing data and the contour plot (see Figure 7-10). We define it in lines 7 through 96 in the *figures.py* module, shown in Listing 7-15.

```
import plotly.graph_objs as go

def serve_prediction_plot(...):
    ...

    # Create the plot
    # Plot the prediction contour of the SVM
    trace0 = go.Contour(
    ...
    )

    # Plot the threshold
    trace1 = go.Contour(
    ...
    )

    # Plot Training Data
    trace2 = go.Scatter(
    ...
    )

    trace3 = go.Scatter(
    ...
    )
```

```
    layout = go.Layout(
...
    )

    data = [trace0, trace1, trace2, trace3]
    figure = go.Figure(data=data, layout=layout)

    return figure
```

Listing 7-15: Creating a graph object and filling it with data

This code skeleton shows how we create the contour plots shown in Figure 7-10 that visualize the SVM confidence levels, as well as the two scatter plots for the training and test data. We store these plots in four variables: trace0, trace1, trace2, and trace3. We then use these variables as the data input argument of the go.Figure() constructor that creates a Plotly figure object containing the four datasets.

We'll take a look at the go.Contour component next.

Creating a Plotly Contour Plot

A *contour line* is a great way to visualize three-dimensional data in a two-dimensional plot. Each point *(x,y)* in 2D space has an associated *z* value, which you can think of as the "height" of the point (for example, an altitude value for a 2D map). All points on a contour line have the same *z* values. Figure 7-10 shows an example of contour lines.

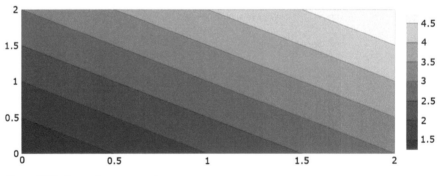

Figure 7-10: Example contour plot

To define these contour lines, we define the *z* values in a 2D array where cell *(x,y)* defines the *z* value for the respective *x* and *y* points in space. Python will then automatically "connect" these points in contour lines. The code snippet in Listing 7-16 produces this plot.

```
import plotly.graph_objects as go


fig = go.Figure(data =
    go.Contour(
        z = [[1, 2, 3],
```

```
            [2, 3, 4],
            [3, 4, 5]]
    ))
fig.show()
```

Listing 7-16: Creating a basic contour plot

In the *z* array, which cells *(x,y)* have a *z* value of 3? The three cells (0,2), (1,1), and (2,0). Now, investigate the contour plot figure and find those points *(x,y)* in 2D space. Is the visualized *z* value the same value of 3?

You can see that by defining a few points with similar *z* values. Plotly does all the heavy lifting of visualizing the contour plot and even coloring it! If you want to learn more about the contour plot (for example, how to customize the *x* and *y* values or the shape of the contour lines), visit *https:// plotly.com/python/contour-plots*.

In the contour plot in the SVM model, the contour lines are the points that generate the same certainty of a point belonging to a particular class. This "certainty" is called a *decision function*, and it associates a value to each point in space. It is the heart of the machine learning model. You could argue that the decision function *is* the model. For a given input *x*, the sign of the decision function *f(x)* defines whether the model *f* predicts that *x* belongs to one class. If it is positive, it belongs to class X, and if it is negative, it belongs to class Y. The more positive or negative the decision function is, the more certain it is that the input point belongs to the class.

Using Dash Loading

In "Using a Dash Graph" earlier, you learned about the dcc.Graph component with the prediction_figure argument. The computations involved are relatively complicated and may take some loading or initialization time. The user may have to wait, and it can hurt usability and feel clunky to use, so the designers of the SVM Explorer app decided to wrap the dcc.Graph in a dcc.Loading component. The idea is simple: while your Python interpreter crunches the numbers and runs the computation, Dash shows you a loading symbol (load spinner). Always keep the user in the loop!

Figure 7-11 shows what such a loading symbol may look like at different points in time.

Figure 7-11: Example Dash loading symbol

This dynamic loading symbol is then shown to the user for as long as it takes to load the Dash component that is wrapped by the dcc.Loading component.

Now let's have a look at how we used the dcc.Loading component in the SVM Explorer app (see Listing 7-17).

```
children=dcc.Loading(
    className="graph-wrapper",
    children=dcc.Graph(id="graph-sklearn-svm", figure=prediction_figure),
    style={"display": "none"},
),
```

Listing 7-17: Setting the loading behavior

The function call has three arguments:

className We associate the graph-wrapper class definition from the CSS stylesheet. This simply defines some width and height constraints for the component.

children This is the dcc.Graph object to be wrapped by the dcc.Loading component. While this object loads, the loading symbol is supposed to be shown.

style We add a dictionary of style attributes to the element. In particular, we set the "display" attribute to "none". This essentially hides the whole element. However, in the stylesheet, we overwrite the "display" attribute to "flex", which sets the size flexibly according to the available space. Code is never perfect, and this could have been written more concisely by the creators of the SVM app.

As it turns out, we won't even see the loading symbol if we run the SVM Explorer app because the components load so quickly. We suspect that this app was initially implemented for a slower version of Dash. But Dash is improving rapidly in speed and usability, so this SVM app can now be computed quickly—and we can simply skip the dcc.Loading wrapper.

For a complete video tutorial on using loading spinners in Dash apps, see the video "Dash Bootstrap Spinner & Progress Bar" available at *https://learnplotlydash.com*.

Dash Callbacks

The SVM Explorer app is an advanced app with many interacting code pieces. So far, we've focused on the isolated components you haven't already seen in another app. Now it's time to look at the bigger picture again, by exploring how the different components interact.

To get a quick overview of where to focus, let's start with the callback graph provided by the Dash framework when you run your app with debug=True (see Listing 7-18).

```
# Running the server
if __name__ == "__main__":
    app.run_server(debug=True)
```

Listing 7-18: Enabling debugging

You can now access the automatically generated callback graph via the button menu shown in Figure 7-12.

Figure 7-12: Callback graph button menu

This button menu should appear at the lower right of your Dash app in your browser. Click **Callback Graph** to obtain what's shown in Figure 7-13.

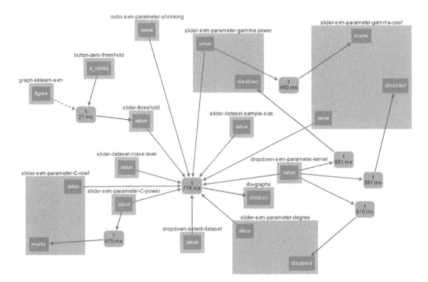

Figure 7-13: The callback graph for the SVM Explorer app

The names above the boxes are the Dash components you defined in your *app.py* file. Listing 7-19 shows an example of the code for a named slider.

```
drc.NamedSlider(
    name="Cost (C)",
    id="slider-svm-parameter-C-power",
    min=-2,
    max=4,
    value=0,
    marks={
        i: "{}".format(10 ** i)
        for i in range(-2, 5)
    },
)
```

Listing 7-19: NamedSlider component definition, showing where the names in the callback graph come from

You can find the name `slider-svm-parameter-C-power` in one of the upper four boxes. With the named slider, you feed into the `slider-svm-parameter -C-coef` component. All components feed into the `div-graphs` component that holds all our SVM graphs.

So, let's focus on the callback function that maps all those inputs into the single output component div-graphs in lines 346 through 453 in the *app.py* main file. In particular, we're going to start with the input and output annotations and the function definition, shown in Listing 7-20.

```
@app.callback(
    Output("div-graphs", "children"),
    [
        Input("dropdown-svm-parameter-kernel", "value"),
        Input("slider-svm-parameter-degree", "value"),
        Input("slider-svm-parameter-C-coef", "value"),
        Input("slider-svm-parameter-C-power", "value"),
        Input("slider-svm-parameter-gamma-coef", "value"),
        Input("slider-svm-parameter-gamma-power", "value"),
        Input("dropdown-select-dataset", "value"),
        Input("slider-dataset-noise-level", "value"),
        Input("radio-svm-parameter-shrinking", "value"),
        Input("slider-threshold", "value"),
        Input("slider-dataset-sample-size", "value"),
    ],
)
def update_svm_graph(
    kernel,
    degree,
    C_coef,
    C_power,
    gamma_coef,
    gamma_power,
    dataset,
    noise,
    shrinking,
    threshold,
    sample_size,
):
```

Listing 7-20: Input and output annotations of the SVM graph

Instead of a single input, the function has a list of inputs, as shown graphically in the callback graph. All those inputs are needed to calculate the SVM model. This SVM model is then used to create all the graphs you see in the SVM Explorer app.

Listing 7-21 shows the code that generates the different graphs.

```
    # ... Model Computations Skipped for Readability ...

    return [
        html.Div(
            id="svm-graph-container",
            children=dcc.Loading(
                className="graph-wrapper",
                children=dcc.Graph(id="graph-sklearn-svm",
                                    figure=prediction_figure),
```

```
                style={"display": "none"},
            ),
        ),
        html.Div(
            id="graphs-container",
            children=[
                dcc.Loading(
                    className="graph-wrapper",
                    children=dcc.Graph(id="graph-line-roc-curve",
                                       figure=roc_figure),
                ),
                dcc.Loading(
                    className="graph-wrapper",
                    children=dcc.Graph(
                        id="graph-pie-confusion-matrix",
                        figure=confusion_figure
                    ),
                ),
            ],
        ),
    ]
```

Listing 7-21: Return value of the update_svm_graph *function that generates the graphs in the SVM Explorer app*

The return value is a list of two Div elements. The first holds the prediction figure discussed in the "Creating a Plotly Contour Plot" section earlier in this chapter. The second holds two more dcc.Graph elements: a line graph and a pie chart. Figure 7-14 shows the three generated graphs.

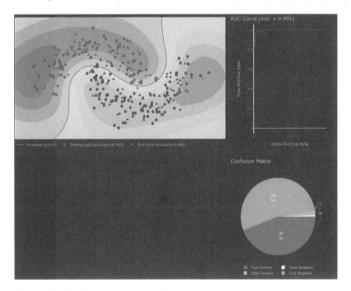

Figure 7-14: Three dcc.Graph elements

Summary

We covered many advanced Dash concepts in this chapter. You learned about the robust SVM classification algorithm and how dashboards can help you visualize machine learning models. You learned how to integrate NumPy and scikit-learn into your Dashboard apps, and how to create reusable components. You also learned about or strengthened your understanding of Dash HTML components such as `html.Div`, `html.A`, `html.Section`, `html.P`, `html.Button`, and `html.H2`, as well as standard Dash components such as `dcc.Graph`, `dcc.Slider`, and `dcc.Dropdown`.

You now possess the skills to go out there and create your own complex dashboard apps and dive into the gallery to learn about advanced Dash components and features. We didn't just give you the fish; we told you how and where to get the fish yourself. The gallery is an ocean full of fish, and if you ever feel hungry for more, you'll know where to go!

Resources

To dive deeper into the SVM Explorer app, feel free to check out the following resources recommended to us by Xing Han, one of the app's creators:

- Classifier comparison: *https://scikit-learn.org/stable/auto_examples/ classification/plot_classifier_comparison.html*
- ROC metric: *https://scikit-learn.org/stable/auto_examples/model_selection/ plot_roc.html*
- Confusion matrix: *https://scikit-learn.org/stable/modules/model_evaluation .html#confusion-matrix*
- SVM classifier (SVC): *https://scikit-learn.org/stable/modules/generated/ sklearn.svm.SVC.html*
- "A Practical Guide to Support Vector Classification (SVC)": *https://www .csie.ntu.edu.tw/~cjlin/papers/guide/guide.pdf*

8

TIPS AND TRICKS

There is still so much more to discover within the rich Dash library. In this chapter, we've put together a few pointers to help you take the next step in your Dash journey. These are tips that we have found helpful as we learned Dash and started building more advanced applications.

We'll take a deeper look at the Dash Enterprise App Gallery, where you can discover open source code used to build more advanced apps within specific industries. You'll also learn to leverage the Plotly community to help you overcome coding bumps along the road. We'll share some Bootstrap themes and debugging tools that will help you embellish your apps and solve bugs. We'll talk you through navigating the dash-labs repository, where cutting-edge Dash features are constantly developed. Lastly, this chapter will offer you a set of Dash learning resources to enhance your knowledge and make programming with Dash even more fun and exciting.

Dash Enterprise App Gallery

As we've mentioned throughout the book, one helpful way to learn about more advanced and complex Dash apps is by exploring the Dash Enterprise App Gallery (*https://dash.gallery/Portal*). Many of these apps are open source, meaning the code is fully available to you on GitHub. To find out whether a particular app is open source, click the information icon located in the lower-right corner of the app card (pointed to in Figure 8-1); a modal should open, and if it says something along the lines of "Unauthenticated: Anyone can access this app," it will be open source. This information card should also tell you which programming language the app uses; a great majority of them are written in Python, as you might expect.

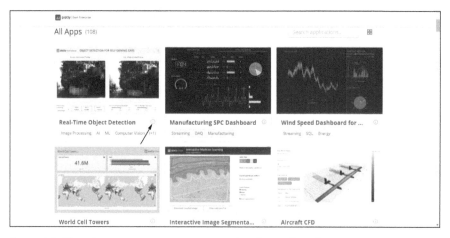

Figure 8-1: The information icon on an app card in the Dash Gallery

The gallery is being added to all the time. To find the apps that are most relevant to your needs, filter the page by clicking a specific industry at the very top of the page. One tip: as you scroll through the apps, think of the layout you want for your own current app project. If you find a particular layout interesting, access the open source code to see if you can replicate that layout in your app.

Enhancing Your Learning with the Plotly Forum

The Plotly forum (*https://community.plotly.com*) is a community forum for both Plotly and Dash. If you don't already have an account on the Plotly forum, you should open one now. Countless times through your Dash development journey, the members of the forum community will help you learn more about Dash and the Plotly graphing library, overcome hurdles, and resolve specific bugs. Even if you don't currently have a problem with your code, we recommend that you take the time to go onto the forum and read a few threads on a topic you'd like to explore. There is so much to learn just by reading about the experiences of other users; most importantly, browsing the forum will help you understand how to create a topic, provide useful answers, and ask questions in a way that will give you actionable answers. You'll soon see how the forum contributes to the growth of the community. Figure 8-2 shows the landing page of the forum; of course, it will look different every time you visit, so it won't look exactly like this.

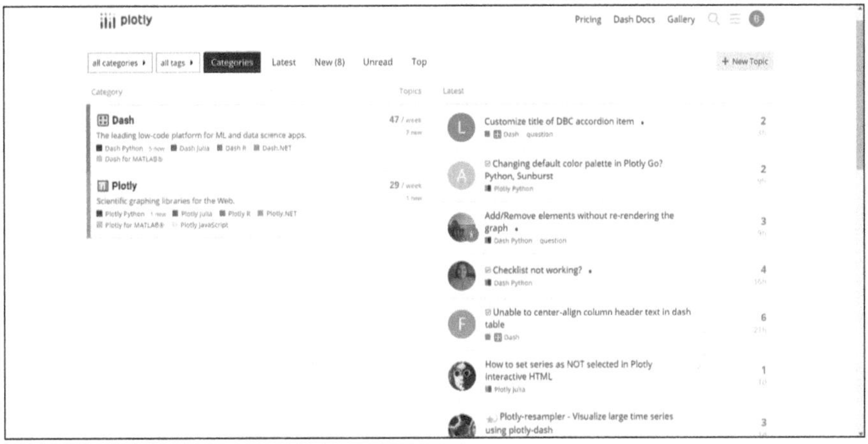

Figure 8-2: The Plotly forum landing page

On the left of the page you will find the main categories, *Dash* and *Plotly*. On the right you'll find the most recent posts for both categories, regardless of the topic.

The community on the forum tends to be very active and helpful. To ensure that your own questions are likely to be seen and answered, always use a post title appropriate for your question and clearly state the problem you're facing; also, make sure you add the code related to your question. This code is often referred to as a *minimal working example*, and it allows potential responders to copy your code and test it on their system to see if they can produce the same problem or error. Make certain that the code is formatted correctly, using the preformatted text symbol </> inside the editing toolbox.

As you gain more experience in Dash, take the time to give back to the community and help others by answering their questions as well. Finally, we encourage you to share apps you create with the community by using *show-and-tell* to tag your posts.

App Theme Explorer

In Chapter 5, you learned how to add Bootstrap themes to your app, like so:

```
app = Dash(__name__, external_stylesheets=[dbc.themes.BOOTSTRAP])
```

These themes will apply only to Bootstrap components in your app. To fully implement a theme into your app, you will need to apply the theme to the Dash DataTable, Dash Core Components, and Plotly figures as well. The *Dash Bootstrap Theme Explorer* at *https://hellodash.pythonanywhere.com*, shown in Figure 8-3, allows you to choose a theme and see how it looks on all the components, text, and figures on the page. To view the available themes, click **Change Theme** on the left side of the page. A panel should slide out with a list of themes. Click one, and take a look at how the dropdown and checklist components, title, text, graph, and DataTable all change in style and color.

Figure 8-3: The Dash Bootstrap Theme Explorer landing page

Choose a theme that suits your app and follow these four steps to add it to all the elements of the app. We'll implement the VAPOR theme within a sample app as our example; find the full *app.py* file in the *Chapter-8* folder of the book's resources at *https://github.com/DashBookProject/Plotly-Dash*.

1. Install the *dash_bootstrap_templates* library and then import both *load_figure_template* and *dash_bootstrap_components*. To do this, open your PyCharm terminal and enter:

```
$ pip install dash-bootstrap-templates
```

To import the necessary libraries, type the following in your main app file:

```
import dash_bootstrap_components as dbc
from dash_bootstrap_templates import load_figure_template
```

2. Add the prebuilt Dash Bootstrap stylesheet to your app and select a theme. Here we chose VAPOR. Make sure you maintain the uppercase style when replacing the theme where Dash is instantiated:

```
dbc_css = "https://cdn.jsdelivr.net/gh/AnnMarieW/dash-bootstrap-templates
@V1.0.4/dbc.min.css"
app = Dash(__name__, external_stylesheets=[dbc.themes.VAPOR, dbc_css])
load_figure_template(["vapor"])
```

3. Incorporate the selected theme into the template prop of the bar graph:

```
fig = px.bar(df, x="Fruit", y="Amount", color="City", barmode="group",
template="vapor")
```

4. Lastly, add className="dbc" to the outer container of the app, as shown in the following code:

```
app.layout = dbc.Container([
    html.H1("Hello Dash", style={'textAlign': 'center'}),
    html.P("Type anything here:"),
    dcc.Input(className="mb-2"),
    dcc.Graph(
        id='example-graph',
        figure=fig

    )
],
    fluid=True,
    className="dbc"
)
```

The *app.py* file used in this example should generate the app shown in Figure 8-4 when you execute it.

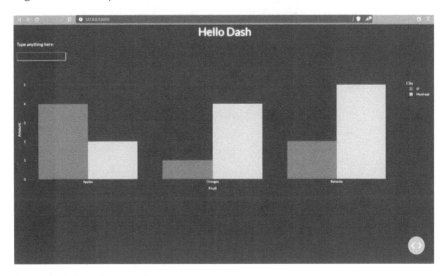

Figure 8-4: Complete sample app

Debugging a Dash App

Knowing how to effectively debug your app will save you many hours of trial and error when bugs occur. Teaching you the full skill set of debugging is beyond the scope of this chapter; however, here we've put some material together to help you get started.

Python has a few options for free debugger packages. For Dash, we recommend the `ipdb` package. To install it, go to your terminal and enter:

```
$ pip install ipdb
```

Let's look at an example where debugging might be helpful. Find the *debug-demo.py* file in the book's code at *https://github.com/DashBookProject/ Plotly-Dash*. When you run it on your computer, you should see something like Figure 8-5. This is supposed to be an app that graphs bill totals over time.

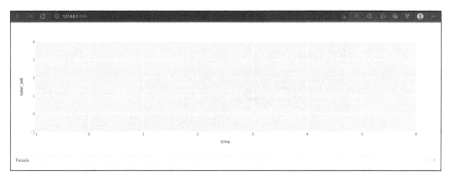

Figure 8-5: The debug-demo.py *app once executed*

This is pretty frustrating: our app doesn't throw any errors, but clearly something is wrong since the graph is not displaying any data. Let's debug our app to find out where the problem lies.

First, uncomment the first line of code in *debug-demo.py* to `import ipdb`. Then activate the debugging feature in the first line of code inside the callback function by uncommenting this line:

```
ipdb.set_trace()
```

You can of course debug any section of the app you'd like; in our case, we'll start at the callback function that builds the graph, since the problem is with the graph. Lastly, turn off the native Dash debugging mechanism and turn off the app's multithreading so that you don't break your session with overlapping `ipdb` instances, as is done in *debug-demo.py*:

```
if __name__ == '__main__':
    app.run_server(debug=False, threaded=False, port=8004)
```

Save and run the altered *debug-demo.py* file and click the HTTP link to open your app in the browser. Going back to the run tool window, you should see something like Figure 8-6.

Figure 8-6: Debugging activated in the PyCharm run window

If you try to execute `print(dff.head())` in the run window, you'll get an error saying that `dff` is not defined. That's because the line of code that creates and defines `dff` is on line 23, which has not been executed yet. To tell the debugger to execute that next line of code, enter a lowercase **n** in the run window. Now, if you execute `print(dff.head())` again, you should see the first five rows of your DataFrame, as shown in Figure 8-7.

Figure 8-7: The DataFrame printed in the run window

However, when you next press **n** to execute code line 24 and enter `print(dff.head())` again, you'll see a notification in the run window telling you the DataFrame is empty:

```
Empty DataFrame
Columns: [total_bill, tip, sex, smoker, day, time, size]
Index: []
```

This is because line 24 filters the day column to only have rows with `'Mon'`. It appears that zero rows have `'Mon'` as a value, which is why the DataFrame is empty. To check what unique values are present in the day column, enter `print(df.day.unique())` in the run window. You'll find only the `['Sun' 'Sat' 'Thur' 'Fri']` values within the day column. That is why the graph did not plot anything when the app was executed: there was no data to plot.

To fix your app, change `'Mon'` to `'Fri'` on line 24 and restart the *debug-demo.py* file. (If your app will not restart, change the port number at the very end from 8004 to anything else.) Back in the terminal, instead of entering **n** for each line of code, you can just enter **c** to continue program execution until completion. Because there is no other bug (breakpoint) in the app, it successfully executes and should look like Figure 8-8.

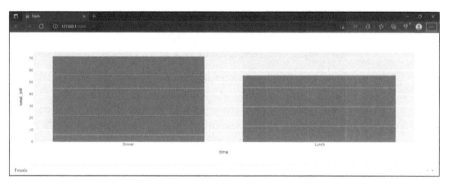

Figure 8-8: The debug-demo.py *app executed successfully after debugging*

For an `ipdb` cheat sheet, go to *https://wangchuan.github.io/coding/ 2017/07/12/ipdb-cheat-sheet.html*.

Happy debugging!

dash-labs

dash-labs is a GitHub repository started by Plotly as a work-in-progress technical preview of potential future Dash features, found at *https://github.com/ plotly/dash-labs*. Community feedback and active participation are essential to the success of this repository because features are built for and with the help of the community. Some features from the past couple of years that were developed in dash-labs include flexible callback signatures (*https:// dash.plotly.com/flexible-callback-signatures*) and long callbacks (*https://dash.plotly .com/long-callbacks*).

At the time of this writing, two active projects in dash-labs include the Multipage Apps feature for a quick and seamless way to write multipage apps and the Dashdown feature to allow execution of Markdown documents with Dash. To start exploring dash-labs, click the ***docs*** folder in the dash-labs repository (Figure 8-9) and read more about the features that have been developed so far.

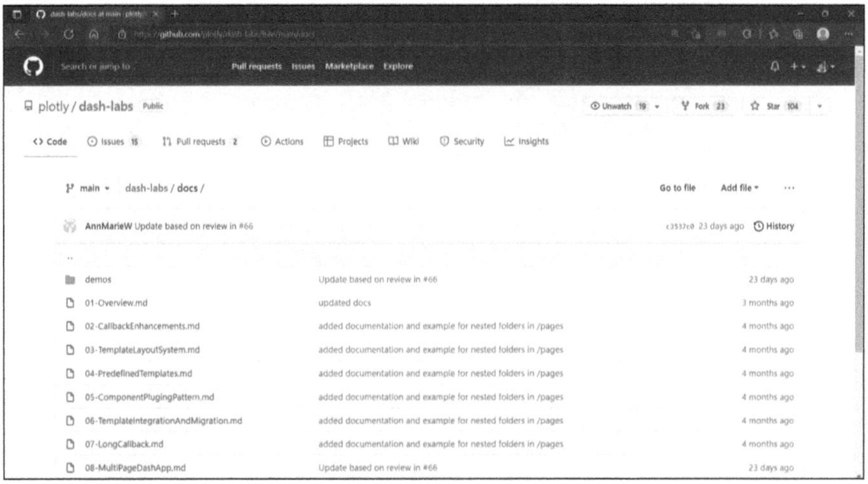

Figure 8-9: The docs *folder pertaining to the dash-labs repository*

To try out some of the features yourself, you can `git clone dash-labs` and run any of the *app.py* or *app_dbc.py* files located in the *demos* folder.

Formatting Your Code with Black

Writing code in a well-formatted manner is not only visually pleasing but also crucial for readability. As you develop your skills, the programs you create will become bigger and more complex. If those programs are not well formatted, you can easily get lost within your own code. Manually formatting your code according to the PEP8 format, which is the official Python style guide, is very time-consuming. Luckily, we have the Python tool *Black*: a code formatter.

Let's see Black in action. Start by installing Black:

```
$ pip install black
```

Then download the *pre-black-formatting.py* file from *https://github.com/ DashBookProject/Plotly-Dash* and open it (Listing 8-1).

```
from dash import Dash, dcc, html
import plotly.express as px
import pandas as pd

app = Dash(__name__)

df = pd.DataFrame({
  ❶ 'Fruit': ["Apples", "Oranges", "Bananas", "Apples", "Oranges",
            "Bananas"],
    "Amount": [4, 1, 2, 2, 4, 5],
    "City": ["SF", "SF", "SF", "Montreal", "Montreal", "Montreal"]
})
```

```
❷ fig=px.bar(df, x="Fruit", y="Amount", color="City")

  app.layout = html.Div([
    html.H1("Fruit Analysis App", style={'textAlign':'center'}),
    ❸ dcc.Graph(
      id='example-graph',
      figure=fig
    )
  ],
  )

  if __name__ == '__main__':
    app.run_server(debug=True)
```

Listing 8-1: The pre-black-formatting.py *file*

There are a few formatting inconsistencies in the code. For example, the Fruit key ❶ is surrounded by single quotation marks while the Amount and City keys are surrounded by double quotation marks. Likewise, the Fruit key values span across two lines of code while the other key values are written out on one line of code. Also, in the line that builds the Plotly Express bar chart ❷, we can see that there is no space before or after the equal sign (fig=px.bar). Lastly, we see that the Dash Graph component is written out across four lines of code ❸, while the html.H1 component, right above it, is written out on one line of code. There are a few more inconsistencies in the code; see if you can spot them before using Black.

To use Black, open the terminal and move into the directory that holds *pre-black-formatting.py*. Once there, enter the command followed by the filename, as shown here:

```
$ black pre-black-formatting.py
```

Black will automatically format the file without renaming it. For the purpose of this demo, we renamed the file to *post-black-formatting.py*, also located in the book's GitHub repository (Listing 8-2).

```
from dash import Dash, dcc, html
import plotly.express as px
import pandas as pd

app = Dash(__name__)

df = pd.DataFrame(
    {
        "Fruit": ["Apples", "Oranges", "Bananas", "Apples", "Oranges", "Bananas"], ❶
        "Amount": [4, 1, 2, 2, 4, 5],
        "City": ["SF", "SF", "SF", "Montreal", "Montreal", "Montreal"],
    }
)

    fig = px.bar(df, x="Fruit", y="Amount", color="City") ❷
```

```
app.layout = html.Div(
    [
        html.H1("Fruit Analysis App", style={"textAlign": "center"}),
        dcc.Graph(id="example-graph", figure=fig), ❸
    ],
)

if __name__ == "__main__":
    app.run_server(debug=True)
```

Listing 8-2: The post-black-formatting.py *file formatted with Black*

We see that all single quotation marks have been replaced with double quotation marks and the Fruit key values are written out on one line of code instead of two ❶, there's an equal amount of spacing before and after the equal sign ❷, and the Graph component is also on one line instead of four ❸. As you can see, the code formatted by Black is consistent and a lot easier to read.

Follow-up Resources

The important thing is not to stop questioning; curiosity has its own reason for existing.
—Albert Einstein

Understanding that learning never stops, we've put together a few resources to help you become an expert in Dash:

- Our very own website dedicated to teaching Dash and sharing updates related to this book also offers a suggested list of videos to watch to deepen your knowledge of Dash: *https://learnplotlydash.com.*

- The Dash Bootstrap Cheat Sheet site, built by our coauthor Ann Marie Ward, offers summaries of the main Bootstrap styling syntax, shortcuts to the documentation on all the Dash Bootstrap Components, and links to different sections of the Dash docs: *https:// dashcheatsheet.pythonanywhere.com.*

- Finxter, a Python educational website with over half a million students monthly founded by our coauthor Chris Mayer, is a great place to learn Python and sharpen your pandas skillset. Go to *https://app.finxter.com.* For free access to Chris's book *Coffee Break Pandas*, see *https://blog.finxter .com/coffee-break-pandas-book-page.*

- Charming Data's YouTube channel and its respective GitHub repository, created and maintained by our coauthor Adam Schroeder, are excellent resources for learning Dash and staying up-to-date with the most recent Dash developments: *https://www.youtube.com/c/CharmingData* and *https:// github.com/Coding-with-Adam/Dash-by-Plotly.*

- The comprehensive list of Dash components created and maintained by the community will allow you to enrich your app with capabilities and features that will make it look more professional: *https://community.plotly .com/t/community-components-index/60098.*

- The following are a few online courses dedicated to teaching Dash and Plotly. Please make sure you read the reviews before deciding which course would work for you:

  - *https://www.datacamp.com/courses/building-dashboards-with-dash-and-plotly*
  - *https://www.coursera.org/projects/interactive-dashboards-plotly-dash*
  - *https://www.pluralsight.com/courses/plotly-building-data-visualizations*
  - *https://www.udemy.com/course/interactive-python-dashboards-with-plotly-and-dash*

APPENDIX

PYTHON BASICS

 The focus of this appendix is to give you a quick refresher on the basics of Python. A full crash course in Python would be beyond the scope of a Dash book, so we'll just go over basics like keywords, data structures, control flow, and functions. There are plenty of excellent resources in the wild that you can use to master Python more fully, including our free email academy: *https://blog.finxter.com/ email-academy.*

NOTE *The introductory section uses code examples and text snippets from* Python One-Liners *(No Starch Press, 2020), written by one of the authors of this book. We encourage you to read the book to obtain a thorough understanding of single lines of Python code.*

Installation and Getting Started

If you don't already have Python installed, you need to set Python up on your computer. Because Python is continuously evolving, we'll keep this information generalized.

1. First, visit the official Python website at *https://www.python.org/ downloads* and download the latest version of Python for your operating system.

2. Run the installer on your computer. You should see a dialog that looks something like the one shown in Figure A-1, depending on the version and operating system. Make sure to click the box to add Python to PATH to allow you to access any directory on your computer via Python.

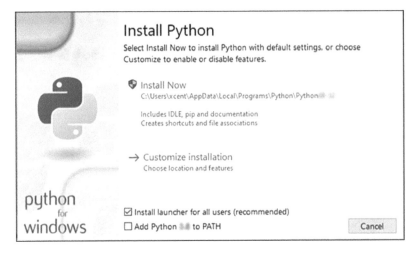

Figure A-1: The Install Python pop-up window

3. Check that your Python installation works correctly by running the following command in your command line (Windows), terminal (macOS), or shell (Linux):

```
$ python—version
Python 3.x.x
```

NOTE   *The dollar sign ($) is just a prompt that signals you to run the following code in a terminal or code shell. The text that follows in bold is the command you should enter.*

Congratulations! You have installed Python on your computer. You can start writing your own programs with the IDLE editor that's built into your system. Just search for the word *IDLE* on your operating system and open the program.

As a first program, enter the following command into your shell:

```
print('hello world!')
```

Python will interpret your command and print the desired words to your shell (see Figure A-2):

```
hello world!
```

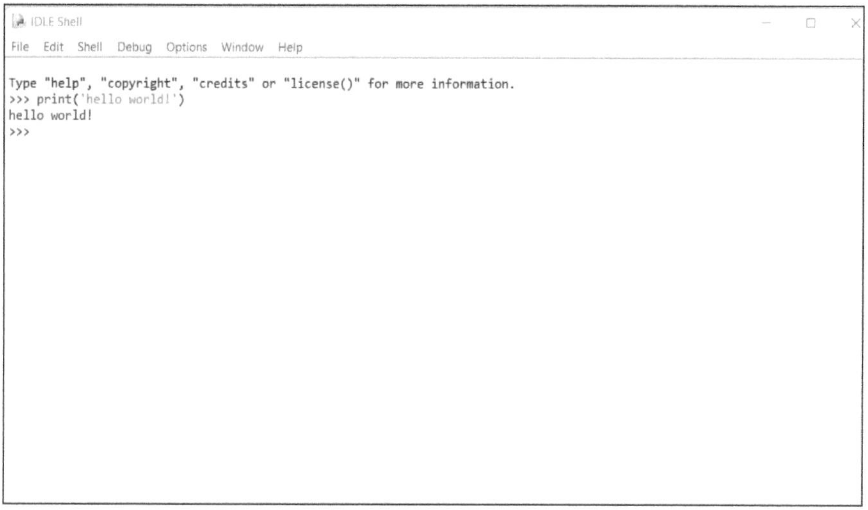

Figure A-2: The hello world program in Python

This mode of communicating back and forth with your Python interpreter is called *interactive mode*. It has the advantage of immediate feedback. However, the most exciting consequence of programming computers is automation: writing a program once and running it again and again.

Let's start with a simple program that greets you by name each time you run it. You can save the program and run it later at any point in time. These kinds of programs are called *scripts*, and you save them with the suffix *.py*, as in *my_first_program.py*, to save them as Python files.

You can create a script via the menu of your IDLE shell, as shown in Figure A-3.

Figure A-3: Creating your own module

Click **File ▸ New File** and copy-paste the following code into your new file:

```
name = input("What's your name?")
print('hello' + name)
```

Save your file as *hello.py* on your desktop or in any other location. Your current script should look like Figure A-4.

Figure A-4: A program that takes user input and prints the response to the standard output

Now, let's get some action going: click **Run ▸ Run Module**. The Python program starts executing in the interactive shell, without you needing to type in each line. It runs through the code file line by line. The first line asks you to put in your name and waits until you enter some input. The second line then takes your name and prints it to the shell. Figure A-5 shows the program in action.

Figure A-5: Example execution of the program in Figure A-4

Data Types

Now that you've seen a Python program in action, we'll review some basic data types.

Booleans

A Boolean data type represents just the keyword False or True. In Python, Boolean and integer data types are closely related, because a Boolean type internally uses integer values: False is represented by integer 0 and True is represented by integer 1. Booleans are generally used for assertions or as outcomes for comparisons. The following code snippet gives you an example of these two Boolean keywords in action:

```
X = 1 > 2
print(x)
# False

y = 2 > 1
print(y)
# True
```

After evaluating the given expressions, variable x refers to the value False and variable y refers to True. Booleans allow us to create conditional execution of code, so they are important for working with data because they allow us to do things like check if a certain value is above a threshold before we use that value (see the SVM Explorer app in Chapter 7 for threshold-based data classification).

Boolean values have a few major operators that represent basic logical operators: and, or, and not. The keyword and evaluates to True in the expression x and y if both x is True and y is True. If just one of those is False, the overall expression becomes False.

The keyword or evaluates to True in the expression x or y if x is True or y is True or both are True. If just one is True, the overall expression becomes True.

The keyword not evaluates to True in the expression not x when x is False. Consider the following Python code example, which uses each Boolean operator:

```
x, y = True, False

print(x or y)
# True

print(x and y)
# True

print(not y)
# True
```

By using these three operations—and, or, and not—you can express all the logical expressions you'll ever need.

Boolean operators are ordered by priority. The operator not has the highest priority, followed by the operator and, followed by the operator or. Consider these examples:

```
x, y = True, False

print(x and not y)
# True

print(not x and y or x)
# True
```

We set the variable x to True and y to False. When calling not x and y or x, Python interprets this as ((not x) and y) or x), which is different from, say, (not x) and (y or x). As an exercise, figure out *why*.

Numerical Types

The two most crucial numerical data types are integer and float. An *integer* is a positive or negative number without floating-point precision (for example, 3). A *float* is a positive or negative number with floating-point precision (for example, 3.14159265359). Python offers a wide variety of built-in numerical operations, as well as functionality to convert between numerical data types. Here's an example of a few arithmetic operations. First we'll create an x variable with the value 3 and a y variable with the value 2:

```
>>> x, y = 3, 2
>>> x + y
5
>>> x - y
1
>>> x * y
6
>>> x / y
1.5
>>> x // y
1
>>> x % y
1
>>> -x
-3
>>> abs(-x)
3
>>> int(3.9)
3
>>> float(3)
3.0
>>> x ** y
9
```

The first four operations are addition, subtraction, multiplication, and division, respectively. The // operator performs integer division. The result is an integer value that is rounded toward the smaller integer number (for example, 3 // 2 == 1). The % operation is a *modulo operation*, which gives you just the remainder of a division. The minus operator - turns the value into a negative number. abs() gives the absolute value (simply the value as a non-negative). int() turns the value into an integer, discarding any numbers after the decimal point. float() turns the given value into a floating point. The double asterisk ** means to multiply to the power of. Operator precedence is just as you learned in school: parentheses before exponent before multiplication before addition, and so on.

Strings

Python strings are sequences of characters. Strings are immutable, so they cannot be changed once they are created; you must create a new string if you want an altered string. Strings are typically just text (including numbers) inside quotes: "this is a string". Here are the five most common ways to create strings:

Single quotes: 'Yes'

Double quotes: "Yes"

Triple quotes (for multiline strings): '''Yes''' or """Yes"""

The string method: str(yes) == 'yes' is True

Concatenation: 'Py' + 'thon' becomes 'Python'

To use whitespace characters in strings you need to specify them explicitly. To start text on a new line within the string, use the newline character '\n'. To add a tab's worth of space, use the tab character '\t'.

Strings also have their own set of methods. The strip() method removes the leading and trailing whitespaces, including empty spaces, tabular characters, and newline characters:

```
y = " This is lazy\t\n "

print(y.strip())
```

The result is much neater:

```
'This is lazy'
```

The lower() method lowercases the whole string:

```
print("DrDre".lower())
```

We get:

```
'drdre'
```

The upper() method uppercases the whole string:

```
print("attention".upper())
```

This gives us:

```
'ATTENTION'
```

The `startswith()` method checks whether the argument you supply can be found at the start of the string:

```
print("smartphone".startswith("smart"))
```

It returns a Boolean:

```
True
```

The `endswith()` method checks whether the argument you supply can be found at the end of the string:

```
print("smartphone".endswith("phone"))
```

This also returns a Boolean:

```
True
```

The `find()` method returns the index of the first occurrence of the substring in the original string:

```
print("another".find("other"))
```

Like so:

```
Match index: 2
```

The `replace()` method replaces the characters in the first argument with the characters in the second argument:

```
print("cheat".replace("ch", "m"))
```

cheat becomes:

```
meat
```

The `join()` method combines all values in an iterable argument, using the string with which it is called as a separator between the elements in the iterable:

```
print(','.join(["F", "B", "I"]))
```

We get:

```
F,B,I
```

The len() method returns the number of characters in a string, including whitespace:

```
print(len("Rumpelstiltskin"))
```

This gives us:

```
String length: 15
```

The in keyword when used with string operands checks whether a string appears in another string:

```
print("ear" in "earth")
```

This too returns a Boolean:

```
Contains: True
```

This nonexclusive list of string methods shows that Python's string data type is flexible and powerful, and you can solve many common string problems with built-in Python functionality.

Control Flow

Let's dive into some programming logic that allows our code to make decisions. An algorithm is like a cooking recipe: if that recipe consists of only a sequential list of commands—fill a pot with water, add the salt, add the rice, get rid of the water, and serve the rice—you might complete the steps in a matter of seconds and end up with a bowl of uncooked rice. We need to respond differently to different circumstances: remove the water from the pot only *if* the rice is soft, and put the rice in the pot *if* the water is boiling. Code that responds differently under different conditions is known as *conditional execution* code. In Python the conditional execution keywords are if, else, and elif.

Here's a basic example that compares two figures:

```
half_truth = 21

if 2 * half_truth == 42:
    print('Truth!')
else:
    print('Lie!')
```

This will print:

```
Truth!
```

The if condition 2 * half_truth == 42 generates a result that evaluates to either True or False. If the expression evaluates to True, we enter the first branch and print Truth!. If the expression evaluates to False, we enter the second branch and print Lie!. As the expression evaluates to True, the first branch is entered, and the shell output is Truth!.

Each Python object, like a variable or a list, has an implicitly associated Boolean value, meaning we can use Python objects as conditions. For example, an empty list evaluates to False and a non-empty list evaluates to True:

```
lst = []

if lst:
    print('Full!')
else:
    print('Empty!')
```

This prints:

```
Empty!
```

If you don't need an else branch, you can simply skip it, and Python will skip the whole block if the condition evaluates to False:

```
if 2+2 == 4:
    print('FOUR')
```

This prints:

```
FOUR
```

The output is printed only if the if condition evaluates to True. Otherwise, nothing happens. The code has no side effects because it's simply skipped by the execution flow.

You can also have code with more than two conditions. In this case, you can use the elif statement:

```
x = input('Your Number: ')

if x == '1':
    print('ONE')
elif x == '2':
    print('TWO')
elif x == '3':
    print('THREE')
else:
    print('MANY')
```

The code takes your input and compares it against strings '1', '2', and '3'. In each case, a different output is printed. If the input doesn't match any string, the final branch is entered and the output is 'MANY'.

The following code snippet takes user input, converts it into an integer, and stores it in the variable x. It then tests whether the variable is larger than, equal to, or smaller than the value 3, and prints a different message depending on the evaluation. In other words, the code responds to real-world input that is unpredictable in a differentiated manner:

```
x = int(input('your value: '))
if x > 3:
    print('Big')
elif x == 3:
    print('Medium')
else:
    print('Small')
```

We give the keyword `if` followed by the condition that determines which path the execution follows. If the condition evaluates to `True`, the execution path follows the first branch given in the indented block that follows immediately. If the condition evaluates to `False`, the execution flow looks further, doing one of three things:

1. Evaluates additional conditions as given by an arbitrary number of `elif` branches

2. Moves into the `else` branch if neither an `if` nor an `elif` condition is fulfilled

3. Skips the whole construct when no `else` branch is given and no `elif` branch holds or exists

The rule is that the execution path starts at the top and moves down until either any condition matches—in which case the respective code branch is executed—or all conditions are explored but none matches.

Here you see that it is possible to pass objects into an `if` condition and use them like Booleans:

```
if None or 0 or 0.0 or '' or [] or {} or set():
    print('Dead code') # Not reached
```

The `if` condition evaluations to `False`, so the `print` statement is never reached. This is because the following values evaluate to the Boolean value `False`: the keyword `None`, the integer value `0`, the float value `0.0`, empty strings, and empty container types. The expression `None or 0 or 0.0 or ''` `or [] or {} or set()` evaluates to `True` if Python can implicitly convert any of the operands to `True`, but here it doesn't because all of them are converted to `False`.

Repeated Execution

To allow for repeated execution of similar code snippets, Python has two types of loops: `for` loops and `while` loops. We'll create a `for` loop and a `while` loop to achieve the same thing in different ways: print the integers 0, 1, and 2 to the Python shell.

Here's the for loop:

```
for i in [0, 1, 2]:
    print(i)
```

This will print:

```
0
1
2
```

The for loop repeatedly executes the loop body by declaring a loop variable i that iteratively takes on all values in the list [0, 1, 2]. It then prints the variable i until it runs out of values.

Here's the while loop version with similar semantics:

```
i = 0
while i < 3:
    print(i)
    i = i + 1
```

This will also print:

```
0
1
2
```

The while loop executes the loop body as long as a condition is met—in our case, as long as i < 3. The choice of which you use depends on your situation. Generally, you'll use a for loop when iterating over a fixed number of elements, such as when iterating over all elements in a list, and a while loop when you want to repeat a certain action until you accomplish a certain result, such as guessing a password until you're in.

There are two fundamental ways to terminate a loop: define a loop condition that evaluates to False, as used in the previous example, or use the keyword break at the exact position in the loop body where you want it to stop. Here we use break to exit what would otherwise be an infinite loop:

```
while True:
    break # No infinite loop

print('hello world')
```

From this we get:

```
hello world
```

We create a while loop with a loop condition that will always evaluate to True because the loop condition while True already is inherently True. The loop ends prematurely at break, so the code moves on and executes print('hello world').

You may wonder why we would want to create an infinite loop in the first place if we don't want it to run forever. This is a common practice, for example, when developing web servers that must use an infinite loop to wait for a new web request and serve the request. However, you'd still want to be able to terminate the loop prematurely. In the web server example, you might want to stop serving files if your server detects that it's under attack. In these cases, you can use the keyword break to stop the loop if a certain condition is met.

It is also possible to force the Python interpreter to skip certain areas in the loop without ending it prematurely. In our web server example, you may want to skip execution of malicious web requests instead of halting the server completely. You can achieve this with the continue keyword, which finishes the current loop iteration and brings the execution flow back to the loop condition at the start:

```python
while True:
    continue
    print('43') # Dead code
```

This code will execute forever without executing the print statement once, because the continue statement finishes the current loop iteration and takes it back to the start before it reaches the print() line. That print() line is now considered *dead code*: code that will never be executed. The continue statement and break are commonly only used with additional conditions using if-else, like so:

```python
while True:
    user_input = input('your password: ')
    if user_input == '42':
        break
    print('wrong!') # Dead code

print('Congratulations, you found the secret password!')
```

This code requests a password and runs forever or until the user figures out the password. If they enter the correct password 42, the keyword break is reached and the loop terminates, sending execution to the successful print statement at the end. In all other cases, the loop breaks, execution returns to the start, and the user will have to try again. Here's a sample usage:

```
your password: 41
wrong!
your password: 21
wrong!
your password: 42
Congratulations, you found the secret password!
```

These are the most important keywords for controlling the execution flow of your programs.

Other Useful Keywords

Let's have a look at some additional useful keywords. The in keyword checks whether a certain element exists in a given sequence or container type. Here we check if 42 is in the list that follows, then whether 21 can be found as a string in the set:

```
print(42 in [2, 39, 42])
# True

print('21' in {'2', '39', '42'})
# False
```

The in keyword returns a Boolean, so the first statement will return True and the second False.

The keyword is checks if two variables refer to the same object in memory. Beginners in Python are often confused about the exact meaning of the keyword is, but it's worth taking the time to understand it properly. Here we see the difference between two variables pointing to the same object in memory, and two lists that look similar but point to different objects:

```
x = 3
y = x

print(x is y)
# True

print([3] is [3])
# False
```

As you can see in the latter example, if you create two lists—even if they contain the same elements—they still refer to two different list objects in memory. If you later decided to modify one list object, this would not affect the other list object. If you check whether one list refers to the same object in memory, the result is False. Here, when we check whether x is y, we get True because we explicitly set y to refer to x. When we check the list [3] against [3], however, we get False because the lists refer to different objects in memory. If you change one, you don't change the other!

Functions

Functions are reusable code snippets that accomplish a specific task. Programmers can and often do share functions with other programmers to deal with specific tasks, saving people the time and effort of writing the code themselves.

You define a function using the def keyword. Here we define two simple functions that each print a string:

```
def say_hi():
    print('hi!')


def say_hello():
    print('hello!')
```

A function consists of the function name with parentheses, prefixed with the def keyword, and the function body, which is an indented code block. This block can contain other indented blocks, like if statements, and even further function definitions. As with any block definition in Python, you must indent the function's body.

Here's a function that prints two strings on new lines:

```
def say_bye():
    print('Time to go...')
    print('Bye! ')
```

Run all three functions in your Python shell like so:

```
Say_hi()
Say_hello()
Say_bye()
```

Here's the output:

```
hi!
hello!
Time to go...
Bye!
```

The functions are executed in order.

Arguments

A function can also take arguments within the parentheses. An *argument* allows you to tailor the output. Consider this function, which takes a name as its only argument and prints a customized string to the shell:

```
def say_hi(name):
    print('hi ' + name)

say_hi('Alice')
say_hi('Bob')
```

We define the function and then run it twice with different arguments: 'Alice' then 'Bob'. Thus, the output of the function executions is different:

```
hi Alice
hi Bob
```

Functions can also take multiple arguments:

```
def say_hi(a, b):
   print(a + ' says hi to ' + b)

say_hi('Alice', 'Bob')
say_hi('Bob', 'Alice')
```

The output is the following:

```
Alice says hi to Bob
Bob says hi to Alice
```

In the first function execution, the argument variable a takes on the string value 'Alice' and the argument variable b takes on the string value 'Bob'. The second function execution reverses this assignment, giving us different output.

Functions can also have return values, so you can pass a value into the function and get back a value that you can then use later in the code, as shown in Listing A-1.

```
def f(a, b):
   return a + b

x = f(2, 2)
y = f(40, 2)

print(x)
print(y)
```

Listing A-1: Using the return keyword

The return value is the expression right after the keyword return, which also terminates the function. Python checks the return value right after the return keyword and ends the function, immediately giving this value back to the caller of the function.

If you don't explicitly provide a return expression, Python will implicitly add the expression return None to the end of the function. The keyword None means *the absence of a value*. Other programming languages, such as Java, use the keyword null, which often leads to confusion when beginners assume it's equal to the integer value 0. Instead, Python uses the keyword None to indicate it's an empty object, like an empty list or string, and not a numerical 0.

When a function finishes executing, the execution is always passed to the caller of the function; the return keyword just gives you more control about *when* to terminate the function and *what* to give back.

We pass a=2 and b=2 into the function in Listing A-1, and get the result 4. We then pass a=40 and b=2 and get the (one and only) answer 42. Here's the output:

```
4
42
```

Almost every dashboard app contains at least one function that adds some interactivity. Commonly, you may have a function that updates a graph based on some user input, something like this:

```
def update_graph(value):
    if value == 2:
        return 'something'
```

Next, we'll look at a more advanced and highly relevant feature of Python: *default function arguments*.

Default Function Arguments

Default arguments allow you to define a function with optional arguments in Python. If a user opts not to provide an argument when they call the function, the default argument is used. You set the default argument by using the equal sign (=) after the argument name and appending the default value.

Listing A-2 shows a more interesting example. Here we define a function add() that returns the sum of the function arguments a and b. So, add(1,2) will return 3 and add(41,1) will return 42. We specify default values for the function arguments: 0 for a and 1 for b. If no value is passed for one or both of these arguments in the function call, it will be set to its default value. So, add(1) will return 2, add(-1) will return 0, and add() will return 1 because the default arguments 0 and 1 are used for a and b.

```
def add(a=0, b=1):
    return a + b


print(add(add(add())))
```

Listing A-2: Defining a function with default arguments

This will print:

```
3
```

In the innermost function call we highlighted in print(add(add(add()))), we call the function add() with no arguments, so it uses the default values for a and b (0 and 1, respectively).

For the remaining two calls, you only pass one argument to add(), and that's the return value of the previous function call. This argument will receive a, taking the position of the arguments to figure out which argument to pass to which variable, and b will have its default value 1. The first, innermost call of add() returns 1. This is passed to add() in the second call and so is incremented by 1, and then that value is again incremented by 1 in the third call.

Here is what happens behind the scenes when we execute Listing A-2, step by step:

```
add(add(add()))
   = add(add(1))
   = add(2)
   = 3
```

You can see that default arguments can help you make functions more flexible in regard to their inputs.

Python Resources and Further Reading

- Feel free to check out the *Python One-Liners* introductory Python videos available for free at *https://pythononeliners.com*.
- The official Python website with the newest Python version for download can be found at *https://www.python.org*.
- You can find a full tutorial on Python lists with detailed video content on the Finxter blog at *https://blog.finxter.com/python-lists*.
- For a full tutorial with video on Python slicing, visit *https://blog.finxter.com/introduction-to-slicing-in-python*.
- You can find a complete guide on Python dictionaries at *https://blog.finxter.com/python-dictionary*.
- A guide on list comprehension with video is available at *https://blog.finxter.com/list-comprehension*.
- An object-oriented programming (OOP) cheat sheet can be downloaded as a PDF at *https://blog.finxter.com/object-oriented-programming-terminology-cheat-sheet*.
- Find more cheat sheets and a free Python crash course at *https://blog.finxter.com/python-crash-course*.

INDEX

Twitter Likes Analysis app. *See* social media analysis app

two-way synchronization, callbacks, 120

type prop, DataTable component, 111

U

update_svm_graph function, SVM Explorer app, 151

upper() method, strings, 171–172

utils folder, SVM Explorer app, 132, 136, 145

V

value prop

    Dropdown component, 61

    RadioItems component, 82–83

    RangeSlider component, 84

viewport, web page, 103

Virtualenv, 21

W

Ward, Ann Marie, 163

while loops, 175–176

whitespace characters, 171

World Bank API

    connecting to, 74–75

    extracting data, 76–78

    identifying indicators, 75–76

World Bank Data Analysis dashboard app. *See* global data analysis app

wrapper functions

    defined, 124, 137

    formatted slider, 139–140

    named slider, 140–141

X

Xing Han, 128, 152

The Book of Dash is set in New Baskerville, Futura, Dogma, and TheSansMono Condensed.

RESOURCES

Visit *https://nostarch.com/python-dash* for errata and more information.

More no-nonsense books from **NO STARCH PRESS**

PYTHON ONE-LINERS
Write Concise, Eloquent Python Like a Professional
BY CHRISTIAN MAYER
216 PP., $39.95
ISBN 978-1-7185-0050-1

PYTHON FOR DATA SCIENCE
A Hands-On Introduction
BY YULI VASILIEV
248 PP., $29.99
ISBN 978-1-7185-0220-8

DIVE INTO ALGORITHMS
A Pythonic Adventure for the Intrepid Beginner
BY BRADFORD TUCKFIELD
248 PP., $39.95
ISBN 978-1-7185-0068-6

MINING SOCIAL MEDIA
Finding Stories in Internet Data
BY LAM THUY VO
208 PP., $29.95
ISBN 978-1-59327-916-5

PRACTICAL DEEP LEARNING
A Python-Based Introduction
BY RONALD T. KNEUSEL
464 PP., $59.95
ISBN 978-1-7185-0074-7

BEYOND THE BASIC STUFF WITH PYTHON
Best Practices for Writing Clean Code
BY AL SWEIGART
384 PP., $34.95
ISBN 978-1-59327-966-0

PHONE:
800.420.7240 OR
415.863.9900

EMAIL:
SALES@NOSTARCH.COM
WEB:
WWW.NOSTARCH.COM

Never before has the world relied so heavily on the Internet to stay connected and informed. That makes the Electronic Frontier Foundation's mission—to ensure that technology supports freedom, justice, and innovation for all people—more urgent than ever.

For over 30 years, EFF has fought for tech users through activism, in the courts, and by developing software to overcome obstacles to your privacy, security, and free expression. This dedication empowers all of us through darkness. With your help we can navigate toward a brighter digital future.

ELECTRONIC FRONTIER FOUNDATION EFF